M000202041

Stepping Into Purity

A Movement of Women

on the Journey from Captivity to Freedom

Where God's spirit is there is
freedom. Enjoy your key
to freedom and love → Jesus!

Stepping Into Purity
Copyright 2020 by Vernicia T. Eure

This title is also available as an eBook. Visit www.verniciateure.com

Scripture quotations marked (ESV) are taken from the ESV® Bible (The Holy Bible, English Standard Version®), copyright © 2001 by Crossway, a publishing ministry of Good News Publishers. Used by permission. All rights reserved.

Scripture quotations marked (KJV) are taken from the authorized (King James) Version. Rights in the Authorized Version in the United Kingdom are vested in the Crown. Reproduced by permission of the Crown's patentee, Cambridge University Press.

Scripture quotations marked (MSG) are taken from THE MESSAGE, copyright © 1993, 2002, 2018 by Eugene H. Peterson. Used by permission of NavPress. All rights reserved. Represented by Tyndale House Publishers, a Division of Tyndale House Ministries.

Scripture quotations marked (NKJV) are taken from the New King James Version®. Copyright © 1982 by Thomas Nelson. Used by permission. All rights reserved.

Scripture quotations marked (NLT) are taken from the Holy Bible, New Living Translation, copyright ©1996, 2004, 2015 by Tyndale House Foundation. Used by permission of Tyndale House Publishers, a Division of Tyndale House Ministries, Carol Stream, Illinois 60188. All rights reserved.

Scripture quotations marked (NIV) are taken from the Holy Bible, New International Version®, NIV®. Copyright © 1973, 1978, 1984, 2011 by Biblica, Inc.™ Used by permission of Zondervan. All rights reserved worldwide. www.zondervan.comThe "NIV" and "New International Version" are trademarks registered in the United States Patent and Trademark Office by Biblica, Inc.™

Scripture quotations marked (TLB) are taken from The Living Bible copyright © 1971. Used by permission of Tyndale House Publishers, a Division of Tyndale House Ministries, Carol Stream, Illinois 60188. All rights reserved.

All rights reserved. No part of this publication may be reproduced, stored in a retrieval system, or transmitted in any form or by any means-electronic, mechanical, photocopy, recording, or any other except for brief quotations in printed reviews, without the prior permission of the author. Send all inquiries to vernicia@-consultinggroup.com.

Cover design: Beyond the Book Media
Interior Design: Beyond the Book Media
Author photos: VA Expressions Photography

First Printing December 2020 / Printed in the United States of America

"Blessed are the pure in heart: for they shall see God."

Matthew 5:8, KJV

TABLE OF CONTENTS

Acknowledgments 7

Preface 11

Introduction 13

PART ONE **20**

Stepping Into Purity 21

Step 1: Confess Your Wrongs to Yourself 25

Step 2: Confess to God 33

Step 3: Acknowledge Your Hurt 39

Step 4: Practice Forgiveness 43

Step 5: Check Your Identity 49

Step 6: Find Security in the Right One 55

Step 7: Recognize Your Need for Affection 63

Step 8: Change Your Environment 74

Step 9: The Break-Up 84

Step 10: Get a Spiritual Mentor 90

Step 11: Study, Recite and Memorize God's Word 93

Step 12: Speak Out Words of Declaration 102

Step 13: Join a Bible-teaching, Christ-centered Church 110

Step 14: Choose God's Best 113

Step 15: Let Freedom Ring 121

Where Do We Go From Here? 126

PART TWO   **131**

Additional Chapters 132

Masturbation 133

Pornography 146

Looking Again 151

More Courageous Faith Stories 160

You Can Do This! 207

More About the Author 210

Acknowledgments

I would like to thank my Abba Father for being a good, good Heavenly Daddy to me. I would not have written this book had He not protected me and brought me out of darkness into His marvelous light. It was He who drew me back to Himself after I wandered away, thinking someone or something was better than Him and the life He planned for me. He knew I was looking for love in all the wrong places. He knew I did not have an accurate estimation of myself. He knew I would fall for all the lines I heard from men and all the promises they would not be able to keep. He knew He was enough for me, but He waited patiently and wooed me until I saw things clearly. He has a plan and purpose to prosper me in every way, and I am thrilled to be on this ride with Him. Lord, I thank you for all you have done for me. You are my everything! I am also, as you know, awaiting that special day when you will bring my handsome husband my way. Until then, you will remain my Heavenly Husband.

***

To my parents, thank you for raising me in a godly home and continuing to point me to Christ. Yes, our God is awesome, and He is always faithful. I appreciate you encouraging me to stay in the faith and serve the risen King. I had a lot of hard-headed years, but I thank God and you two for being patient and merciful towards me. Your leadership did not go in vain. I love you!

I would also like to thank my siblings, my niece, my extended family, and the best friends I could ever ask for. You all are my cheerleaders and I appreciate your love and support!

I want to thank Tiphani Montgomery, a woman of God and entrepreneur extraordinaire, for saying "Yes!" to God. She planned a prophetic writing retreat at her first Millions Conference in 2017 and gave the audience an outline for writing this book. Also, one of the retreat speakers, Sophia Ruffin, told us to voice record the content to make it easier. I told my roommate that I was not leaving the conference without writing this book. I went up to my room after the VIP session and voice recorded the book in thirty-five minutes. When I arrived home, I turned on the voice memos on my phone and played them in front of my tablet, which dictated the words in a Google document. The rest is history. To God be the glory! Many others have had their hands in this process. I am grateful to all who contributed financially to this project as well as my family and friends who have prayed for me and pushed me along to finish this book. Thanks for checking on me and making sure I did not quit.

To the Courageous Faith Writers who shared their stories in this book: Thank you so much for being my beautiful, brave sisters. More women will walk in freedom and truth after hearing about your experience. You are simply amazing!

To my writing coach, Tracee Garner (author), thank you for your guidance and encouragement along the way. You are the best! To my editors, Gina Johnson (author) and Felicia Murrell—thank you for the hours you spent on making sure this book read well. To Chanel Martin (author), Jacinta Martinez, and the Beyond the Book Media team, thank you for your professional publishing services. I could not have done this without you.

To my sisters in the *Stepping Into Purity and Beyond* (SIP) group on Facebook: When I created "The SIP Group," your presence gave me the motivation to keep going. I wrote this book for you and other single women who will be joining our group. Thank you for your sisterhood, authenticity, and desire to continue succeeding as beautiful women with healed hearts and transformed lives.

To June Elliott, my former volunteer at The Keim Centers: Years ago, you told me, "I see a long line of women behind you. They are waiting for you." I've never forgotten that. Thank you for speaking into my life with boldness and wisdom. I can see it clearly now.

PREFACE

I CAN'T LIVE WITHOUT SEX! Many women feel that way. Can you relate? I certainly can. I was the woman who longed for intimacy with a man, the woman who felt like I couldn't live without a man's affection and companionship, and the woman who was miserable because I was living outside of God's perfect will for my life. Is that you? If so, you did the right thing by picking up this book. This book is for the single woman who is no longer finding pleasure in having sex outside of a marital covenant. Right now, you may not be able to imagine your single life without sex, but I am here to tell you that there is a vibrant and full life you can live without sexual activity. Beyond the implementation of the principles in this book are freedom and transformation, release from the guilt and shame that comes from living a double life, sexual purity, and the perfect peace that your heart desires.

If you are like me, you open a book, look at the table of contents, pick the chapter of interest according to the current season of your life, and begin reading. I read short snippets that I can apply to my life, and you can do that with this book too. Or, you can read the book from cover to cover; it is your choice. Regardless of how you read this book or what you choose to read first, my prayer is that you find freedom from the bondage of sexual sin and experience a transformation in your mind, body, soul, and spirit.

Before you get started, let me make one thing clear. You will not read any condemnation throughout these pages. If you do, please understand it is not my intent to shame you. I am here to empower you to live the life of freedom God designed for you. My desire is for you to experience love, grace, acceptance, affirmation, validation, forgiveness, strengthening, encouragement, understanding, freedom, transformation, and peace. I also pray that you will not feel alone on this journey. As you learn more about me and the women who have shared their stories, know that as you take each step, we are here with you and for you. Sister, you are not the only one struggling and held captive by your own destructive choices. There is a whole movement of SIP sisters who get it. We were where you are now, and although a few of us are still in the midst of the struggle, we all know that there is tangible hope on the other side. We've seen it in many situations in our lives.

Today, you can decide that you want better for your heart and for your life. Believe that you can change your course right now.

Can you see us taking each step with you?

Take courage and hold out your hand.

We will grab it and walk with you.

We are here to help you!

INTRODUCTION

I remember my past life like it was yesterday. Hiding out. Doing what brought me glory. Ducking the "saints" at church. Living like consequences were not going to show up one day. Gratifying all the desires of my flesh and doing just the opposite of how my parents taught me. If I told you half of the careless decisions I've made, you would not believe it. I was undeniably rebellious and operating on autopilot. No one could tell me anything. I was ensnared in the temporal pleasures of the world, serving the evil one while professing to be a Christian. Blinded by the enemy, I was in a dark bottomless pit that I dug so deep I could not see my way out. As a matter of fact, at one point, I did not desire to change. I was having too much fun. The problem was, in that pit, I felt numb to my purpose. I had no desire to discover God's plan for my life. I was too busy seeking euphoric episodes of carelessness. I wanted those moments to last forever because it made me feel wanted, secure, loved, approved, and valued.

God knew what it was going to take to get me back to Him. He never left me alone when I was out there living for myself and serving sin. Do you want to know how I know? Because I felt guilty the whole time. The Holy Spirit was gnawing at me, signaling me to surrender to His will and lay down my own, but my ears were plugged, my eyes were closed, and my heart was hard. I knew my lifestyle was wrong, but I could not bring myself to correct it. Furthermore, I had no desire to change for a long time.

After a few bumps and bruises, I began to miss something essential in my life, P-E-A-C-E. This lifestyle was burdensome. The fun diminished, and the partying got old. I became burdened about things that did not bother me before, and when it came to men, I was tired of the heart-shattering moments of disappointment. The adventures I thought I was experiencing ended in destruction, and the excitement I once experienced no longer made me happy. I was unfulfilled and desired more out of life than what I was living. I was thirsting for the abundant life Jesus created for me. I did not know it at the time, but this was going to be the only thing that filled the void in my life—not my current path of destructive behavior. Life seemed pleasurable back then, but deep down inside, I was feeling empty, hungry for more, fearful, and at times, anxious. I did not recognize that the consequences of my choices were going to be an assault on my future. My party-filled lifestyle morphed into the past that haunted me for years. Unfortunately, today, I am still paying for the consequences of my reckless behavior.

When I started seeing the repercussions of my behavior, I wanted to escape this lifestyle, but I honestly could not see my way out. I remember telling a friend about my struggle. She said, "You can't try to quit everything before coming to God; you have to bring it all to Him. You are not going to be able to stop in your own strength." I said to myself, *I am not going to God with all this mess.* I was embarrassed and felt it was my job to clean it up.

After walking with Christ consistently and counseling hundreds of women who walked a similar path, I realized that we think with our natural minds when it comes to repentance. We believe since we were the ones who messed up that we have to take responsibility to clean up our own mess. And if we don't clean it up, we are dumping our mess on someone else, which is being irresponsible. Nothing is further from the truth.

God knew before the foundations of the world were laid that we did not have enough willpower or strength to correct our own sinful behavior. He knew we needed someone greater to pay for the sins we were going to commit. So, God had a brilliant idea to send His Son Jesus down from His Heavenly home to stand in our place and be crucified for the sins of everyone in the world. Jesus took on the wrongful behavior of man. He died a brutal death for us and was buried in a tomb. He overcame all of our transgressions – past, present, and future. Then, unbeknownst to the folks who killed Him, the unthinkable happened. A woman went to the tomb looking for His body and found that He was gone. Vanished. What could have happened to Him? Later, she found that by the power of Almighty God, Jesus was risen from the grave. Jesus defeated death. This is significant because today, Jesus is alive and hears our prayers. He intercedes on our behalf. He prays prayers for us that we are unable to articulate. God offers abundant life here on earth and eternal life through His Son Jesus Christ. This is the GOOD NEWS for the world!

You may not be able to rescue yourself from sin, but Jesus can save you. If you do not already have a relationship with God, He wants a relationship with you. He loves you beyond your comprehension. In fact, God is crazy about you! He is excited about the gifts He has for you and those placed inside of you. He has a purpose and plan for your life and can't wait for them to be lived out. He does not want your reckless behavior to separate you from Him. Will you trust Him to be your Lord and Savior today? You do not have to wait. If this is what you desire, pray this prayer or one similar to it:

God,

In the powerful name of Jesus, I come to you today, asking you for a new life. I know I have done so much against you. I have not pleased you in every area of my life, and I feel bad about it. I want a life with you. I want to trust you to be my Lord, the Ruler of my life, my Savior, and the Rescuer of my life. I don't know all the details of what this means, but I know I want You, and I need You in my life. I believe that your Son died on the cross for my sins, was buried, and rose from the grave. I believe that having a relationship with You will be an adventure that will change my life forever. I trust that You will show me how to live, protect me from my enemies, and teach me how to live out my purpose and tell others about You. Lord, I believe that once I leave this earth, after completing my work, I will spend eternity with You.

In Jesus' Name, Amen."

If you already have a relationship with the Lord, you can pray:

God,

In the powerful name of Jesus, I come to You today, confessing my sins before You. I ask You for a restored life. I know I have done so much against you. I have not pleased You with my lifestyle, and I feel bad about it. I really need you, and I want to sincerely trust you to be a Lover, Deliverer, and Ruler of my life. I believe that You can change my life forever if I yield to you and not to temptation. I trust that you will show me how to please You. Please strengthen my will and help me to walk in repentance, never to purposely sin against you in this way again. And Lord, if I fall again, please catch me in your mercy and kindness. Teach me how to consistently live out the purposes and plans You have for my life.

In Jesus' Name, Amen.

God rescued me when I did not have a desire to be rescued. He wooed me, and He can do the same for you. The desire to live to please God began to plague my heart. I was no longer interested in partying, getting tangled up with men who just wanted sex, or listening to the same type of music. I wanted to be in right standing with God.

I re-dedicated my life to the Lord several times until I gained traction. This was a pivotal season in my life. God strategically placed people around me at different points to draw me closer to Him. Whether it was something they said or the way they lived, He was beginning to steer my attention to people who successfully lived to please Him.

I remember when He directed me to a job where one of my childhood friends hired and mentored me for almost two years. We did not know that our relationship would be used to grow me spiritually, but now when I look back, that is exactly what God had in mind. This friend trained me in a technical skill, turned me on to different genres of godly music, and shared constructive feedback on my lifestyle lovingly. Presently, we are close friends and serve as a trusted resource for one another. I had no idea this Divine encounter would change the trajectory of my life for the next twenty-plus years.

I would love to say that I did not have any time of regression, but that would be far from the truth. Many times, I reverted to unhealthy behaviors that did not affirm God's perfect plan for my life. However, as I was burdened by these sins, I began unashamedly talking to the Lord about them. I recall crying my heart out and telling God that I did not want to live this way anymore. I feared that I was going to return to my old ways, but God's grace was sufficient for me. As I took my burdens to Him, He began changing my heart all the more. Something shifted, and I got tired of going to Him confessing the same thing. This was getting old. As a result, I planned to conduct myself in a manner in which I did not have to go back to God and keep saying I am sorry. I am grateful that God taught me then and is still teaching me that He wants to hear my thoughts, feelings, dreams, desires, sorrows, and joys. It is His delight to spend time with me and see His purposes fulfilled in my life.

I encourage you to take all of your tainted thoughts, jacked-up emotions, fractured heart, repeated failures, and unbroken cycles to Him. Take your confusion, fear, desires, wants, needs, and dreams to Him and lay them all at His feet. He wants all of it. At this point, you have nothing to lose.

PART ONE

STEPPING INTO PURITY

For the woman who wants to escape her current circumstances, I am aware that this book's title, *Stepping Into Purity,* can be intimidating, to say the least. So, I applaud you for being willing to read this book.

Who likes change and awareness of faults, anyway? Let's face it. Most of us do not rush to find out the issues underneath the smile we put on our faces every day. Digging up those things that are buried below the surface takes work, but I believe you can do it. Issues such as denial, insecurities, infatuation, strong desires, and broken hearts and dreams are all a part of life but can also be a part of our detriment.

I am sharing a peek behind the curtain of my life to lead you through each step you should take to get out of the captivity of sexual sin into long-lasting freedom in Jesus Christ. For a long time, I saw the word *purity* as a bad word. It was something I felt guilty about because I kept falling into sin. It was a word that haunted me because I was not living the way God designed me to live. When I asked one of my inspirational friends for her insight on this topic, this is what she said comes to mind when she thinks of the word purity:

"When I think of purity, I think of things that come in to contaminate the heart. So, when we think of children, purity comes to mind because they are innocent and, for the most part, remain free from a guilty conscience. To me, this is what it means to walk in purity. It is a continuous check with the heart to see if any ways in you would lead to unfulfilled behavior patterns. It is being responsible for your own soul work and finding solutions that will help you release toxic beliefs. It's a completely surrendered journey towards self-love. We begin in life with some sense of purity. This is a path that leads us to reconnect to that part of ourselves, a glorious path we are all worthy of exploring." ~ Tanya Gould

Purity, as defined in the Merriam-Webster dictionary, is freedom from dirt, impurities, sin, or guilt. At this point in your journey, it is essential to remember that while it may not be easy to remain mentally and physically pure, with your commitment, a community of trusted women, and most importantly, with God on your side, it is possible. You will not be able to persevere in your own strength. I believe if you want to be out of bondage, once you ask your Savior Jesus wholeheartedly, He will deliver you from everything that does not please Him, including sexual sin. If He did it for me, He surely can do it for you.

Aren't you tired of sneaking around? Living a secret life? Saying you believe one thing but living contrary to your actual design? Going through heartbreak? Seeing yourself in a constant cycle with men or with yourself? It stops here today.

You can be free from captivity if you want to be. I will be with you throughout the process of being set free from the snares that keep you from receiving all of your God-given inheritance. You don't want to miss this. You are not as far away from freedom as you may think. I promise you I am going to give you the recipe to live a life of victory. Your heart will not be able to handle the same old lifestyle as you read this book. You will find yourself thirsting for more of what God has in store for you than the temporary pleasure you can get on your own.

Your results are dependent on how diligent you are at implementing the principles in this book and taking action on the recommendations. These principles will not render you a quick turnaround because it will be uprooting some deep dark cemented issues that have plagued your soul for many years, but I can promise that you will see results. You will not be alone in this process. If you don't see any changes after following the steps in this book, feel free to contact me so that we can work it out together. I am confident that I can provide the counseling you need to get on the other side of this struggle.

Remember, Jesus is here fighting for you. I am here and will pray with you the whole way. Do not be afraid. Be courageous. Are you ready? Grab a new journal, your favorite pen, and a Bible. Let's go...

STEP 1

Confess Your Wrongs to Yourself

If we are ever going to experience breakthroughs from unhealthy habitual sins, we have to face them and admit something is wrong in our lives. This brings a higher level of awareness to issues that need to be resolved and is an invitation for us to participate in the healing process.

As children of the Living God, we have the Holy Spirit inside of us. When we are living a sin-filled life, He is grieving, and therefore our spirit is in despair. For years, I lived like this. I was a fugitive, running around trying to find love in all the wrong places and hoping to feel that deep intimate satisfaction again. But I was not going to ever find satisfaction in anyone apart from Jesus Christ alone. No one could take His place in my heart. No one.

When we as women are in this place of absolute disobedience, our spirits testify that something is not right. It leads us from a place of discomfort to spiritual despondency. We need our hearts jumpstarted, and only Jesus has the jumper cables.

This is a grace-filled reminder that God made me from dust. He knew Adam and Eve were going to trust their own judgment, opening a pathway for sin to enter not only their lives but the entire world. Therefore, He was well aware that my sinful nature would lead me away from His perfect plans. His compassionate character is what draws us to bringing these things to Him instead of trying to fix them ourselves.

I am not saying this gives me a license to do whatever I want; it doesn't. But it encourages me to extend grace to myself because God does this for me. His grace is sufficient for us. In Him, when I am weak, I am strong. God's *dunamis* power is made perfect in my weakness (2 Corinthians 12:9-10, NIV; emphasis added). Who am I to withhold grace from myself?

Confessing your faults to yourself is one of the most powerful tools you possess. It will release you from being crushed under the enemy's feet. He wants you to stay in denial because He knows if you can see your mistakes clearly and understand that it is safe taking them to God, a breakthrough is coming. There is no doubt that the enemy wants you to remain in bondage, not be freed from it.

If you find it challenging to face your habitual sins, it is entirely reasonable to want to be in denial, ignore the Lord's tugging, and stay right where you are. Your flesh and the enemies of your soul do not want you to live a lifestyle that honors God. This is part of the reason our sinful nature is a problem. It holds us hostage to entrapments and keeps us from fulfilling our purpose. I know because I was there for a long time, and if I am not careful and prayerful, I could revert to this denial again. I do not want to produce fear in you, but I warn you that we have to first be freed. Then we must maintain our freedom in Christ. We cannot sleep on the enemy; we have to be alert and sober-minded. For the enemy is like a roaring lion, seeking whom He may devour. We must resist him and stand firm in the faith. (1 Peter 5:8-9b, ESV).

Have no fear. Since God wants you free, He will be the one to protect you from your enemies. Be assured that "the Lord will fight for you; you need only to be still" (Exodus 14:14, NIV). Psalm 46:10b (NKJV) encourages us to, "Be still and know that I am God." As you are still and allow God to take you through this process, you will see His power show up in your life. "Listen for God's voice in everything you do, everywhere you go; He's the One who will keep you on track" (Proverbs 3:6, MSG).

Let's park right here for a quick moment. Know this - you are not alone in this part of your journey. I am with you, and God wants to be with you too. That is if you want Him to be. He gives you a choice. To His children, He promises in Hebrews 13:5b (NIV), "Never will I leave you; never will I forsake you."

The first thing you need to do is confess your wrongdoing out loud to yourself. I have provided a sample story and a place where you can write out your confession. If you run out of space, turn to another page in your journal. Remember, God wants to be with you in this. It will be imperative that He is with you since satan is lurking around trying to find a weak point in your life to defeat you while you are going through this process. Even if you begin a downward spiral in your thinking and emotions, tell God about it. Do not process the flood of thoughts by yourself. Invite God to participate in this with you. He is ready and willing to accept your invitation.

For example:

Rhana lived outside of God's perfect will for her life. It started when she met Tye at work. She felt an attraction to him but tried to ignore it. He was married, and she knew any future with him was off-limits. Rhana said she had never been tempted in this way before and decided to keep it to herself. The first time she was close to kissing him, she was stunned. It surprised her when it actually happened.

When Rhana looked back on her decision, she tried to figure out how it all transpired; everything moved so quickly. She said, "I was trying to remember if it was me who leaned forward first or him. I felt guilty afterward because I knew he was a married man, but now I think it was my hormones that led me to get into a position where this could happen." Afterward, she knew it was wrong and was disgusted with herself. She felt horrible.

Rhana told a friend about what she had done and asked for prayer. Her friend prayed, and then she prayed, promising God that she would never do it again. Later, she ended up back in the same situation with Tye. Distraught, she cried out, "Lord, help me. Forgive me!" Rhana was trying to break this cycle but found it hard. She was facing a tough situation but was determined that she was not going to always be in this struggle. Again, she confessed her sin to God and trusted Him to free her from this bondage.

Your turn:

"I have had sex outside of God's perfect will for me which is within a marital covenant between a man and a woman. It started when .... (you fill in the blank). The first time I thought .... and I felt ....at the time, but now I think it was .... and now I feel .... "

Take two minutes to confess anything out loud that came to mind as you used the above example. If you get stuck, write it first and then read it.

In my experience, we, as human beings, can easily deceive ourselves into thinking that our wrongs are not all that *wrong.* When deceived, we can justify our behavior and camp out in the river of denial. It happens. Believe me, I have been there more times than I want to admit. This is the reason it is imperative to confess this out loud to yourself.

The truth of the matter is we have sinned against God, the other person, and ourselves. Staying in denial is like telling God that our plan is better than His, which we know to be far from the truth. When we fall into sin, we are acknowledging a need we have and devising a plan to provide for ourselves instead of looking to God to satisfy our desires and fill the void in our hearts. Taking on the provider role offends Him.

1 Corinthians 6:18 (NLT) tells us to "Run from sexual sin! No other sin so clearly affects the body like this one does. For sexual immorality is a sin against your own body." Remember, as daughters of the Most High, "we are God's masterpiece; He has created us anew in Christ Jesus so that we can do the good works He planned for us long ago" (Ephesians 2:10, NLT). God created us in His image and likeness (Genesis 1:27, KJV). Yes, we are a piece of the Master. He designed each one of us with a specific purpose in mind, and if we allow ourselves to be polluted by the lust of the flesh, we will not be able to accomplish those good things.

Yet even when we offend God, the Bible says, "If we confess our sins, He is faithful and just and will forgive us our sins and purify us from all unrighteousness" (1 John 1:9, NIV). He will have compassion on us, trample our sins under his feet, and throw them into the depths of the ocean. (Micah 7:19, NLT), enabling us to walk in freedom and abundance. Who does not want that?

You may have heard this phrase *confession is good for the soul*. I agree confession is a proper cleansing of your soul.

For two more minutes, close your eyes and take a few deep breaths. Inhale through your nose, count to four and hold for four counts. Now, exhale through your mouth for four counts. Then say, "*I forgive myself for the wrong I have done to* .... *[name those that came to mind]. I am created in the image and likeness of a loving God who cares deeply for me. I am free, and God is going to use my freedom to bring glory to Himself and freedom to others.*"

Good job. This is a significant accomplishment. Feel free to repeat this deep breathing exercise at any point throughout this book.

***

Write down your takeaway from this Step and how you plan to take action:

....

....

....

....

STEP 2

Confess to God

G od is loving and kind, and He is a safe place for you to confess your sins. If that comes as a surprise to you, you probably have an incorrect perspective of Him. This is not unusual because we do not see God with our physical eyes. Also, if we are not under the leadership of a pastor who teaches God's Word accurately, we tend to make up in our minds what He is like. Instead, we can ask Him to reveal His nature to us and read His Word to see how He treated others.

I remember feeling like God was this big person in the sky sitting on a throne, looking down, rebuking and correcting me every time I did something wrong. Part of the reason for this was probably due to me actually doing something He did not like. Guilt was sounding an alarm inside, and it made me feel fearful and disconnected from God. Through this open door, more fear entered my life, and it became an idol that would control me for years to come.

I wish I had believed in God's power yet His gentleness during that time. He is mighty yet caring. He is capable of overseeing everything on earth, yet He is attentive to each of us. He is just, yet He is merciful. He is the all-wise God, yet He is humble. He is all-knowing, yet He is patient. He is a mighty warrior and a fighter, yet He is my Lover. He is a Defender, yet He is a meek Shepherd. He is the soon coming King, yet He is present with us right now. He is the Lion of Judah, yet He is lowly. He is Master, Savior, Deliverer, Redeemer, Rescuer, Father, and Friend. Our God is a Restorer and will take the fragmented pieces of your life and mend them back together again.

Know that you can confess anything to God and ask for restoration. He wants to be involved in every detail of your life. You have to know who He really is to feel safe with Him. Open your heart and allow Him to teach you instead of going off of what your imagination conjures up on its own. Ask Him, "Who are you, Lord? Reveal yourself to me. Who am I to you? How do you feel about me? What do you think about me?" You will be surprised at what He says. He will reveal Himself to you, and your identity will be firmly planted in Him instead of in people, places, things, status, and your accomplishments.

Do not forget that you are safe with God at all times. He said, "This is my command – be strong and courageous! Do not be afraid or discouraged. For the Lord your God is with you wherever you go" (Joshua 1:9, NLT). With that said, I had to learn that God knew me and my problems better than I did. It was a waste of time to try to fix my problems myself. I had to give it to God and let Him fix it for me.

Years ago, my friend inquired about my spiritual life, and I shared a laundry list of things that I was not doing right. I knew God was not pleased with the things I was doing, but I felt like I could not stop. I needed to get myself together before returning to Him. My dear friend told me that I could not fix myself before returning to God. She said I needed to take all of my mess to the Lord. This was difficult at first, and I felt like I was shoveling my trash onto God's heavenly driveway and standing there saying, "Now, you clean it up, Lord." I felt ashamed. I thought it was my responsibility to clean up, not God's.

However, if I am going to say I am a believer in Jesus Christ, I have to take Him at His Word and trust what He says. Here are some verses that encouraged me to do this:

> "Praise be to the Lord, to God our Savior, who daily bears our burdens" (Psalm 68:19, NIV).

> "Casting all your cares [all your anxieties, all your worries, and all your concerns, once and for all] on Him, for He cares about you [with deepest affection, and watches over you very carefully" (1 Peter 5:7, AMP).

Maybe you feel like that too. You are not alone in the assumption that you are supposed to fix things before going to the Lord. I hear my clients say this all the time, *"I'm not ready." "I have things I'm still doing, and I don't want to commit and then mess up again."*

Perhaps you are ashamed of the mess you are in and the things you have done. Let me tell you this - God *can* handle it. All He wants you to do is bring all of it to Him. Remember, He is God, and He knew before the beginning of time what things you would struggle with, the crazy decisions you would make, and the many promises you would break. Yet, He still sent His one and only Son to take your place on the cross and die a shameful death just for you and me.

I say to you today, give your mess to God. Write down all the things you can think of that you need to quit, even the things that you don't want to give up right now. Release it to Him.

1. ....

2. ....

3. ....

4. ....

5. ....

6. ....

God,

I have to admit this is uncomfortable for me. I know the things I have written here have offended You, and it makes me sad to even confess them. I am trusting that as I have written each one, You are willing to forgive me for all that I have done, even the things I cannot remember. I want You to bring to my memory the things that did not come to mind so I can confess those as well. I am asking You to forgive me for all the sins I have committed and for ignoring You when you have told me to do something. I want an obedient heart. I want to be in an intimate relationship with You that is on good terms. I am frustrated with myself because I want to obey You, trust You more, and have faith that moves mountains, but I find myself struggling to do right. It makes me frustrated at myself. Would You come into my situation and make things right? I have come to the point in my life where I know I am unable to do right without You working in my heart. Father, thank You for being compassionate, slow to anger, quick to forgive, and for having inseparable love for me. I appreciate You for being patient and not giving up on me. You are the only person that I will have an eternal relationship with who will never change. Thank You, Lord, for Your mercy.

**

Write down your takeaway from this Step and how you plan to take action:

....

....

....

....

STEP 3

Acknowledge Your Hurt

After you've admitted your wrongs and confessed them to God, you must identify wrongs that have been done to you. This is not to dwell on them and allow bitterness to seep in but to acknowledge that someone hurt you and process how you felt about their offense. An offense can be poisonous to the soul. It can eat your loving and kind spirit alive, leaving nothing but sadness, negativity, cynicism, loneliness, and ultimate hopelessness.

Offense builds a fence around you with high walls preventing any penetrable good from getting in. You prevent yourself from rotting inside by admitting there was a wrong, by stating what you think about it and how you felt about it. Then, renounce anything that they gave you that was not yours, take back anything they took from you, forgive the person, release them, and bless them.

1. ....

2. ....

3. ....

4. ....

5. ....

6. ....

Here is an example: I forgive Kevin for acting like he was committed to me while he was having sex with another woman. I knew something was off but did not understand exactly what was going on. I should have known he was not faithful. This frustrates me, and I feel sad because I put years into this relationship and thought we were going to get married. I am furious at him for disrespecting me and not being courageous enough to come talk to me. I am also disappointed with myself. I should have said something when I thought he was cheating, but I was scared. This is not the first time a man has cheated on me, and I was left to figure it out. Sigh.

Sample prayer:

Lord,

I am so tired of being left with the short end of the stick. I can't believe it happened to me again! I thought I did everything to guarantee that I would pick the right guy who would not cheat on me. My heart hurts. (pause and breathe)

Please give me the strength to forgive, release, and bless Kevin and not harbor resentment towards him. I take back all the spiritual, emotional, physical, relational, and mental connections that I gave to him that were designated for me and my husband. I give back to him all the spiritual, emotional, physical, relational, and mental connections that were designated for him and his wife. Show me the value and worth you have assigned to me. Help me, Lord. Help me to walk in the freedom you planned for me. Give me strength and wisdom to avoid the same mistakes over and over again. I desperately need self-control so that I don't mess up again. Teach me how to trust my instincts, see the red flags, and make better relationship choices that honor You. Amen

Maybe your prayer sounds a little different, but regardless, God hears it. I hope that in doing this, you felt a weight lift from your shoulders. The burden is now gone, in the Name of Jesus. You should feel relief. If you do not, ask the Lord to reveal to you the reason you still feel burdened. Perhaps you need to process more hurt with Him. Don't be afraid to spend the time it takes to do this. It is imperative that you rid yourself of this weight so you can experience the freedom God designed for you.

I do want to acknowledge that we will encounter hurtful situations in our lives that we cannot control. The upside of this is that God is there for us. He saw it coming, and He can get us through it. Here's some good news from the writer of Psalm 66:18-20 (NLT), "Come and listen, all you who fear God, and I will tell you what He did for me. For I cried out to him for help, praising him as I spoke. If I had not confessed the sin in my heart, the Lord would not have listened. But God did listen! He paid attention to my prayer. Praise God! He did not ignore my prayer or withdraw his unfailing love from me." When we confess our hurt to the Lord, He will hear our prayers, come to our rescue, and bring the love and healing we need to get back on our feet again.

Sis, God is for you, and don't ever forget it.

***

Write down your takeaway from this Step and how you plan to take action:

....

....

....

....

....

....

STEP 4

Practice Forgiveness

Sprinkled throughout the last three steps, I talked about confession and touched on forgiveness. Now, I would like to amplify the importance of practicing forgiveness and doing it regularly. Increasing your prayer life will be instrumental in keeping your heart pure as well as practicing forgiveness to God, yourself, and others. Enter into a lifestyle of forgiveness by asking God for a pure heart. This allows you to see life from God's perspective. Matthew 5:8 (KJV) says, "Blessed *are* the pure in heart: for they shall see God." When we have a pure heart, we are blessed and can see life from God's perspective. That's a double blessing!

Forgiving Yourself

I pray this when I am approaching God's throne of grace, "Create in me a clean heart, O God, and renew a right (loyal, NLT) spirit within me" (Psalm 51:10, ESV). Typically, we are more aware of asking God and others for forgiveness than we are aware of the extremely important need to also forgive ourselves. We must admit to our mistakes and failures and release ourselves from the things we have done wrong. No one is perfect here on earth. We all mess up. Once we forgive ourselves, we can note the lessons and commit to doing things differently in the future.

We have done a lot of exercises so far, and here is another one to add to this process of *Stepping Into Purity*. In your journal, draw a line down the middle of the page. On the left side, write down all the things you have done in intimate relationships that have negatively impacted you.

For example:

Five years after making a commitment to be abstinent until marriage, I had sex with ....
....*(man's name(s)).*

On the right side of the paper, beside your confession, match it with a forgiveness statement and scripture.

Here's an example:

I forgive myself for not honoring God in my relationship with ....*and violating my commitment to abstain from sex until marriage. Lord, "Wash me clean from my guilt. Purify me from my sin."*

Forgiving Others

In addition to extending forgiveness to yourself, you must forgive, release, and bless those who have betrayed you (See the sample prayer in Step 3). You want to be sure that you are walking in a spirit of forgiveness. If you are holding grudges toward other people, keeping them hostage in your mind and heart because you are still mad at them, you will not be able to experience freedom and receive all that God has for you. Harboring unforgiveness means they remain handcuffed to you. You cannot move forward to your life's destinations and desires if you are refusing to let go of hurt and pain.

Isaiah 61:1 (NLT) says we are people who release the captives and free the prisoners; we don't hold on to them. We allow them to experience the freedom that Jesus died for. This is not easy, and it does not at all ignore the harm that has been done. They will have to answer for their behavior. However, forgiveness is a just act that God has shown us by His example of forgiving us. It's like He's saying, *"I know you did that, but I am not going to hold you to your actions. I am a kind, just and merciful God, and I am going to let you go free. I know you've been made from the dust of this sinful world; therefore, I have pity on you."*

The reality is that people are not perfect, and neither are we. There are boundaries that are necessary to avoid being hurt repetitively by the same people. Prayer and counseling are available to heal our hearts. As Christians, we have a duty to live out Ephesians 4:32 (NKJV), which admonishes us to be kind and tenderhearted to one another and forgive one another even as Christ has forgiven us. Here's a warning. If we are not willing to forgive other people, the Lord God is not going to forgive us, and we cannot afford not to be forgiven (Matthew 6:15, NLT).

Take a moment and turn to a new page in your journal. Pray and ask the Lord to reveal all the people you are holding hostage due to an offense. Write down the names. Keep writing until you have them all listed. Ask the Lord to bring to mind anyone you've omitted. More people may come to mind later, that's okay.

Sample prayer:

I forgive .... for ....
....
......I thought .... and it
made me feel ....
I forgive him, I release him, and I bless him. Amen.

Whew! Take a breath...Ok. This may have been hard but it is behind you now and you are one step closer to freedom. Let's continue.

Even when you have been hurt, you must pray to forgive, release, and bless these individuals who betrayed your trust, abandoned you, lied, cheated, and broke their promises to you. Go one by one and forgive each man for the specific wrong he did. If you are not there yet, do not feel pressured to say it. God understands, and the last thing we want to do is pretend. If you are stuck on a certain person, put a star by their name, and move on. You can come back to them later. Check off the names that you feel confident you can forgive right now.

Ask for Forgiveness

While doing this exercise, ask God for the courage to make amends with anyone on this list that you need to call. He will give you the spirit of humility and fill you with boldness so you can apologize and ask for forgiveness.

Over the years, I have contacted a few men from my past to sincerely apologize for my ungodly behavior. I desired to move on with a clean slate. I wanted to own my part and take responsibility for my actions, and because of my history with some of them, I felt the godly thing to do was to seek their forgiveness. I was nervous, and they were surprised, but I had so much peace doing it.

In addition, if the Lord reminds you of something you have done toward Him regarding these situations, confess it and ask Him to cleanse you of all unrighteousness. We talked about this in Step 2. Remember, you can keep it real with the Lord. He knows what you have done anyway. There is no shame going to Him and having a heart to heart conversation. He wants us to do this, and when we do, we will leave with an abundance of peace. 1 John 1:9 (NKJV) says, "If you confess your sins, God is faithful and just to forgive you of your sins and to cleanse you from all unrighteousness." Psalm 51 is also a good chapter to read to start your prayer with a clean slate. God is willing to release you from the harm you have done to Him, and He is faithful to show you how to do the same for others.

***

Write down your takeaway from this Step and how you plan to take action:

....

....

....

....

STEP 5

Check Your Identity

Listen to me closely on this step. It is vitally important to know who you were made to be. Your very identity can be lost when you are so consumed with someone else that you have no idea who God made you to be and what He designed you to do. This is a danger zone because you can get sucked into a dark place and have trouble finding your way out, especially if you are with someone who is clueless about who He is too, or just downright full of Himself. What God designed us for can get lost in someone else's journey when we become so physically, mentally, and emotionally bonded to the person. As a result of this loss of focus, our top priority shifts to desperately feeling wanted, safe, valued and needed. Some of us even find ourselves entangled in the erroneous belief that we are only valuable and worthy if we have romantic love in our lives. I felt this way for a long time and eventually faced the fact that this is far from the truth.

There were times when I got lost in a man's goals and dreams. His pursuits seemed more exciting than mine. He was making connections, attending business events, growing in his creative skills, and wanted to talk about it with me. I, having a counselor's heart, fascinated with his journey and not focused on the creative things God wanted to do in my life, could sit and listen to his dreams for hours. It was intriguing.

My excitement birthed a strong desire to help him in his endeavors, and this became my focus. I was there to support him. I would come up with ideas for him and wait before planning my schedule to see what he had planned. I was ignoring the fact that I had my endeavors to pursue. As a matter of fact, the more I delved into His interests, the more mine faded away.

This taught me a critical lesson: It is imperative that I have my own life and embrace my own identity before helping someone else. God has purposed for me to do exciting things too, and I needed to give my time to those things instead of someone else's dream.

If I asked you to describe your identity, what would you say about yourself? I am not asking about what you do. I want to know who you are. Take some time to think about this.

If you are having some trouble with describing yourself, consider this. Knowing God is knowing who you are. Not knowing God is not knowing who you are. Period.

When we lose focus, it can cause us to become enmeshed in the dreams of the other person instead of discovering our identity and pursuing the plan God has for our own lives. In situations like these, a relationship imbalance occurs where the person we are with is not returning the same amount of dedication that we are pouring into the relationship. Here's the bottom line: You are who God created you to be, just like you are. You have talents, gifts, likes, dislikes, a personality, and even distinct fingerprints that no one else in the world has but you. He knew you before the foundations of the world were laid. He saw your unformed body. God knitted you in your mother's womb. You are uniquely and wonderfully made by God. No one compares to you in all the world. Everything that God made was good. Your very identity is based on you being created in the image and likeness of Almighty God. This should make you jump up and down and shout out loud joyfully because if I wanted to be like anyone, I would want to be like God Almighty. And the more time we spend with Him, the more we begin looking and behaving like Him.

As we are heirs of God and joint-heirs with Jesus, we have an inheritance that He has provided for us. That means we can "have the mind of Christ" (1 Corinthians 2:16b, NLT) and behave like Him. Our identity comes from our Heavenly Father, who loves us unconditionally, and nothing can separate us from His love (Romans 8:35-39, NLT).

God is not the angry guy in the sky that is pointing His finger at us and making a tally of every wrong that we do. That is not the God we serve. God is a loving and kind Father, and He is always motivated by love. This does not mean that He agrees with the wrongs we do. He does not. Continually ignored and progressive sin gravely hurts Him and can anger Him. However, God is merciful. He does not give us what we deserve. He is the epitome of love. He is also just. This means He is "unbiased, upright, virtuous and righteous" (Google dictionary). Because He is full of mercy, abounding in love, and forgives our sins, we can trust that as we are in the family of God, we are covered by God. As long as we co-operate, He can bring us to a walk of consistent obedience.

The problem lies when we step outside of His plan; it puts us in harm's way, and our true identity becomes marred. I've heard this anonymous quote said before:

A fire inside of a fireplace is warm, cozy, beautiful, and romantic. It's safe, and no harm is anticipated. You can rest in front of it. However, a fire outside of the fireplace destroys. It's hot, it can burn you, it is unsafe, and it is ultimately destructive.

There is no peace in this situation. Marriage is the fireplace, and hot sex can be safely enjoyed within a marital covenant. However, sex outside of marriage destroys a person's identity, reputation, integrity, and relationship. It benefits us more than anyone to live a righteous life, so we don't have to live the consequences of our wrongdoing.

God designed you in a way that is unique to others around you. If you're looking around at other people's lives and comparing your life to theirs, I want to stop you right there. God designed you differently for a reason. He thoughtfully had your purpose in mind, and He wants you to live it out well. Embrace everything about yourself and get to know who you are and whose you are.

Here is another exercise you can do as you are reading through this Step. Stand in the mirror and tell yourself, "*I love you. God loves you. God values you, and He designed you for an exciting purpose. He paid a big price for you, and you are worth a lot to Him.*"

What other personal affirmations can you write for yourself:

Affirmation #1: ....

Affirmation #2 ....

Affirmation #3 ....

Too often, we get invested in someone else's goals and dreams, encouraging them along the way instead of encouraging ourselves and living out our identity and purpose. God has unique attributes that are a perfect fit for our personality, and He will make us stand out in the world like a shining star as we embrace who He created us to be. When I am lost in someone else's dreams or comparing myself to others, it makes me ungrateful for the way God made me. When I do not recognize and appreciate who I am, it is an insult to God because He created me for His glory. One of the best ways we can honor God is to discover the treasures He placed inside of us and fearlessly live out our identity.

***

Write down your takeaway from this Step and how you plan to take action:

....

....

....

....

STEP 6

Find Security in the Right One

As a single person, specifically a Christian single, it will be essential for you to know whose you are and understand that you are safe with God and valuable to Him. When assuming God's unstoppable love for us, we can be secure in knowing that when we are His children, we get access to everything that is His. Furthermore, when we follow His plan, it is worth every sacrifice we are going to make.

Proverbs 3:5-6 (NLT) says, "Trust in the Lord with all your heart; do not depend on your own understanding. Seek His will in all you do, and He will show you which path to take." We can trust God to be there for us, never leaving us alone to figure life out by ourselves. We can trust Him to protect us and provide everything we need. He will show us the way. He will love us through hard times and will never let us go. We can trust Heavenly Father to be our Companion, Helper, Counselor, and Friend.

Write down an experience you have had when God counseled you along the way:

....

....

....

....

....

....

God knows when we are empty and lonely for love. Jeremiah 31:3-4 (NIV) says, "I have loved you with an everlasting love; I have drawn you with unfailing kindness. I will build you up again, and you, Virgin Israel, will be rebuilt. Again you will take up timbrels and go out to dance with the joyful." John 3:16 (NKJV) says, "For God so loved the world that He gave His only begotten Son, that whoever believes in Him should not perish but have everlasting life." Know that there is absolutely nothing that can separate us from the love of God that is in Christ Jesus (Romans 8:38, NLT). Nothing.

Many other verses in the Bible speak to God's secure love for us. God's love cannot be compared to any other love. His love is even greater than a mother's love for her child. His love is not based on feelings; it's based on the fact that He cannot lie. When He says He loves us, He means it. When the Apostle says nothing can separate us from God's love, he is saying there is not one thing on this earth that we can do that will make God stop loving us. What a relief!

I hope you get it now. God's love for you is secure, and it is permanent. His love is grand. It is unstoppable. This provides you the confidence in knowing that if you can trust in God and know that He cannot lie, then you can be secure in knowing that His love is - more than enough for you.

That does not mean you don't need the love of people, specifically a man. God works through humans to reveal His love and then calls them to love other people. Sometimes that is done well, and the love of a man or woman reflects God's perfect love. Other times, people struggle to emulate His love accurately. Again, God's love cannot compare to the love of a human being. Humans are limited in their ability to love. God is unlimited in his ability to love perfectly. His love never fails, and it never runs out even when the love of humans runs short.

The times I have felt insecure are the times that I did not recognize God's place in my life as my King, Lover, Protector, Defender, and Provider. This lack of security made me feel anxious and uncertain of myself. These were times when my perspective was not rooted in who God was in my life, but was rooted in the man in my life that I was trusting to assign value to me and serve as my safe place. In other words, having a man in my life meant I was desired, cherished, and worthy. I did not feel like I was loved if there was not a significant other in my life who spent time with me, held me in his arms, and told me he loved me and needed me. When I had a man in my life, I felt more confident and valuable, but what I was experiencing was a false sense of security.

I did not consider that before the foundations of the world were laid, God had already declared my value and my worth. He planned a purpose for me to be on the earth and to do great things through His power. He assigned me to parents who were going to raise me in a Christian household to grow up to be a leader, author, speaker, counselor, and missionary. I was of great worth to God because He said so. As long as I was rooted in my faith in Him, I was safe with Him, never to be forsaken. This was the truth, but I was not aware of it.

There are situations when I have felt afraid of not being protected, and I was right in that assessment. I was not safe, and God was trying to warn me. I did not have confidence in God's role in my life as the One who sustains me. Bottom line, I lacked security in the One who made me, the One who wanted me to walk in wholeness, not brokenness.

The point is, if I know without a doubt God created me, loves me unconditionally, and sees me as important to Him, then I know when I am in His will, I have nothing to worry about. I am safe with Him, and I can be sure of His promise to me. "I will never [under any circumstances] desert you [nor give up or leave you without support, nor will I in any degree leave you helpless] nor will I forsake or let you down, or relax My hold on you [assuredly not]" (Hebrews 13:5b, AMP).

This assures me that my God will not, in any way, leave me in need. He will not lose His grip on me, and He will not let me fall. That, my friend, is a faithful God.

To further emphasize His devotion to us, Zephaniah 3:17 (NIV) says, "The Lord your God is with you, the Mighty Warrior who saves. He will take great delight in you; in His love, He will no longer rebuke you, but will rejoice over you with singing." God is in hot pursuit to secure us in His love and keep us from danger.

Ways I Have Implemented These Truths in My Life

After living outside of God's will for years and feeling ashamed about it, I now know that I can tell Him anything. I can discuss my frustrations, doubts, fears, and insecurities. I can share my concerns about the hang-ups and strongholds I have, in addition to all the areas where I lack obedience. I can even share my far-fetched dreams and joys with Him. My secrets are safe with God. After all, He knows me. He knows how I think, and He knows how I feel and how I will respond in every situation. Because of God's sovereignty, He already knows every decision I am going to make and what will impact my decisions. He already knows how my life is going to turn out. He knows the beginning from the end. He is aware of the twists and turns in my life, both now and later on down the road. Because of this knowledge, I can depend on Him to warn me when I get into dangerous situations. With Him, I can live free from danger or threat.

Just at this moment, you may have thought that we are not necessarily free from danger because we live in a fallen world. I thought the same and want to remind you that as a child of God, we have been adopted into His family and therefore have access to the inheritance He gives His children. The central part of that inheritance is eternal life with Him in heaven. If we live forever in heaven with Him after this life, then even if harm comes to us on earth, we will not experience that threat for eternity.

Going back to where I was before, God has warned me of dangerous situations in the past. Proverbs 6:5 (NIV) says, "Free yourself, like a gazelle from the hand of the hunter, like a bird from a snare of the fowler." God used this scripture years ago to warn me of a man I dated so that I could escape the relationship. I had prayed and asked the Lord to let me know if this person was someone I should be involved with, and I gave him a time limit to tell me – 30 days. I did not expect the Lord to answer me so soon. He answered in a few days. That was one of the quickest prayers He had answered in a long time. Although I delayed for a short time, I am grateful He told me to run.

That is not the only time He rescued me from a potentially dangerous situation. God has delivered me from many snares in my life and has given me the opportunity to escape situations that would not have been the best for me. There were times I needed rescuing because, in my pride, I thought I knew everything and did not need God for anything. That was so far from the truth. 1 Corinthians 10:13 (NLT) teaches us that when we are tempted, God will show us a way out so we can endure. He gives us an out to keep us safe from harm.

More importantly, just as a good heavenly Dad would do, He allows us to get out of situations before we even get trapped if we will only acknowledge Him and trust him to direct our path.

There have been times when I have asked God to tell me something, but when He gave me the answer, I did not want to listen and went with my own decision. And how many times have you, like me, went on and made your own decisions only to find yourself in a mess?

When we pray and trust God to direct our steps, we should be trusting that His direction is best because He loves us and would never put us in harm's way. He is not emotionally distant. He is always ready to help in times of trouble (Psalm 46:1, NLT). God is a loving Father, and any loving father takes it upon himself to protect his child. Because I am his daughter, I can be secure in knowing that my God is amazingly in love with me. He is a jealous God and wants me to have a safe and securely abundant life with Him here on earth.

Following Christ frees me from the decision to choose my own way. He gives me a choice of going my own way or following His way. I need to listen and be willing to follow His direction to be safe and secure. We can all rest assured that God will never let us down. It is alright for us to fully trust Him, knowing that it is His nature to bless us. He is trustworthy. Humans may let us down, and we may let them down, but God never will fail us.

***

Write down your takeaway from this Step and how you plan to take action:

....

....

....

....

STEP 7

Recognize Your Need for Affection

We all need affection. God made us this way, and He uses others to fulfill that desire in us. Sometimes affection is fulfilled in healthy ways, and sometimes it is not. People often seek affection through sex. While affection can be a part of sex, there can be times when sex excludes true love and affection. Let's pause right here.

If this is your experience, you are not alone. As you read the courageous faith stories at the end of this book, you will find that other sisters did not choose to have this desire for sex; it was forced on them. I say to you today, sweet one, that abuse was not your fault. You did not ask for it in any way. There is a way to freedom. Keep reading.

There are many other reasons a woman will begin having sex. Perhaps you started having sex because you were not getting the affection you needed. And if your love language is physical touch like mine, the absence of affection may seem even worse. Getting the affection you need makes one feel safe, loved, wanted, accepted, and valued.

However, when you desire more affection for a man than what God has designed for you to have in this season, this is when the following problems arise.

Problem 1: Premature love: stirring up love before it's time. "Young women of Jerusalem, I charge you: do not stir up or awaken love until the appropriate time" (Song of Solomon 8:4, HCSB).

Problem 2: You may mistake someone's affection as true, authentic, unconditional love, and devotion when it is not.

Problem 3: You can go quicker and further in the relationship than you planned. Be sure to know the signs of premature entanglement.

Problem 4: You can develop memories and emotional soul ties that may stay with you for the rest of your life.

Your turn:

Problem 5: ....

Problem 6: ....

Problem 7: ....

Many other problems may arise, but these are a few to consider. And I am not saying that showing affection will definitely lead to sex, but it can if you do not set firm boundaries at the beginning of your relationship and commit to sticking with them. Remember, affection is not bad in and of itself. It is a healthy, God-given need for someone to receive appropriate affection. However, it can be misused.

Affection has to be shown in a way that will not tempt you or the other person to cross boundaries. Speaking of boundaries, if you do not set your standards based on your core values before you get in a relationship and discuss them at the beginning of a relationship, you will cross the line.

What are your core values? ....
....
....

The problems I mentioned are self-explanatory but let's go back to Problem 2 and expound on it. When affection goes too far, this speeds up the process of getting to know the person, and it is probably going to lead to a sexual encounter. Premarital sex puts blinders on you and eventually puts scales over your eyes. The blinders only allow you to see what's in front of you and skew your sight of who the person really is and could prevent you from knowing how you think and feel when you are with them. Introducing the person to your loved ones is beneficial because they don't have blinders on. They can see things you cannot see and warn you accordingly. These trusted people can see a wolf in sheep's clothing. They can anticipate whether the relationship will be beneficial to you. If you do not listen, you are taking a gamble on the person's love for you and may even become the obstacle to the real love your heart desires.

Rushed encounters could produce a fabricated relationship with someone who has not betrothed themselves to you, putting you at risk of having your heart crushed into pieces. I had to find this out the hard way. The lesson I learned was that real love was not equal to a good warm hug, quality time, the best sexual partner, or the sweet promises whispered in my ear. Once I began to get to know God and His true love for me, I understood that His love is the all-sufficient eternal love I needed and have always desired. Besides, knowing His love taught me how to recognize real love when it came my way. Real love is sacrificial. It's honest, it protects, and it is ultimately a safe place.

The bottom line is...God made sex for marriage, and anything that is done outside of God's perfect will leads us to other decisions that displease Him. However, there is an upside to this. Choosing a lifestyle of sexual purity alleviates us from living the consequences of sexual sin.

Let's Talk About Sex

God made sex and sex is good. Let the church say, "Amen!"

Not enough people talk about this fact or even know it. They think sex should be separate from God but it was His idea. Sex is sacred and God designed it for a husband and wife to enjoy. We will dive deeper into this as you continue reading. So, now that we have laid this groundwork, let's build on it.

Ladies, every month, your body ovulates in preparation for carrying a pregnancy. When you have sex, you are putting yourself at risk of becoming pregnant outside of a marital covenant. When this happens, some women are so caught off guard and desperate to escape their circumstances that they allow fear to lead them right to an abortion clinic. This may not have been their plan, but as the saying goes, *if you fail to plan, you plan to fail*, and this may not be something a woman ever wanted to happen in her life. For the last 16 years, I have worked with women who are distraught when they see those two lines on the pregnancy test. They had devised a plan of protection by getting on birth control and never thought it would happen to them. As careful as they tried to be, they ended up pregnant anyway. It was not in their plans to have a baby at this point in life but now they are left with deciding which pregnancy option to choose: parenting, adoption, or abortion. Not only that, but many women contract a sexually transmitted disease, are emotionally scarred for years and have mental images that are difficult to overcome. One thing is for sure, you can't put a condom over your heart. Consequently, heartbreak is sure to come when we do not follow God's plan.

This was a surprising reality for me. I had no idea my sexual encounters would put me in jeopardy of having dreams about my ex-boyfriend for years. These were not necessarily romantic dreams, but I was frustrated that he was in them. I wanted to move on and forget about this relationship but my memory held me captive and I needed to find the path to freedom. Have you experienced these unwanted reminders of your past too?

God intended for us to bond sexually through holy matrimony and become one (Matthew 19:5, NLT). Our spouse is marked on us forever. We may not understand this in the physical sense, but spiritually, God's plan was for us to only bond this way with our husband. This union provides security in our relationship where we can freely express our sexuality through intercourse and enjoy companionship the way God intended without the interruption of thoughts from past sexual partners.

Oxytocin and vasopressin are chemicals produced in your body when you have sex with someone. God has placed these chemicals in our bodies for us to bond with another individual. It's like glue, and when trying to separate, it becomes painful and ultimately leaves a print on the other person in which they were bonded. This bond was designed to keep the man and the woman together in marriage. Marriage is much bigger than we even understand, and sexual intercourse is equally important. Sex is God's gift for married people; not for single people. If we have a gift for our future spouse and take that gift and use it outside of God's perfect design for a husband and wife, we are cheating ourselves of having the peaceful and enjoyable life God planned for us.

As a married person having sex within God's plan, there are safety measures God has placed there. However, having sex as a single person could be dangerous and detrimental to your life. Emotional instability could rise. Your life has to be well thought out, and that is what has to be considered to live the abundant life Christ came to give us.

As a single woman, if you are seeking affection you are probably in need of intimacy too. The intimacy you are seeking when you are having sex with someone is the intimacy God can offer. Let intimacy with Him be your foundation and launching pad for a successful marriage. This is what you are really looking for. Then when you are married, God can show you how to become one with your spouse because you are already one with Him. This is a desire only He can meet. Do you believe God can provide the affection and intimacy you need in a healthy way that brings glory to Him? If you have never seen Him provide for you in this way, ask Him. You will be surprised. He can also provide for your emotional needs.

We tend to feel secure when we receive affection from the arms of another individual, but the only real security we have is with God. He is the only One we have a sustained eternal relationship with after this life is over, and He knows what we need. Our earthly relationship with people will end. So investing in our eternal relationship with God would be even more beneficial to us.

God created us for a purpose, and He has plenty of plans to fulfill that purpose. He desires for us to live the life He designed specifically for us. In following His plan, there we find security. God knows what we need, and when we have urges to have sex, He absolutely understands. We can tell our heavenly Daddy, the Designer of our bodies, all about it, and He will provide for us in ways that we have never imagined. He can supply us with the abundance of love, power, and self-control we need to honor Him.

If you are struggling with having sex outside of marriage and want to be free, you can be free today. If you are looking for more in life and you have not been able to find it, or if your heart has been crushed over and over again, you're probably disappointed in yourself and feel empty inside. Know that you can turn to God your Creator, and He will reveal His purpose to you so you can live a life that honors Him. A life that He will bless tremendously.

Affection is not a bad thing to desire. However, when we try to obtain it in a way that God has not designed for us, it will cause lifelong ramifications that are difficult to overcome. To overcome this, look for healthy ways to receive affection. You can volunteer in the nursery for the children's program at church. You can hug a friend or your parents. Spend some time with an elderly person who has loved you since you were a child. Receive healthy affection by being around affectionate family, friends, and children. Pray for God to prepare you for marriage and send you a spouse.

Let God know that you need affection. I am confident He will send people who will wrap their arms around you and make you feel safe. But more importantly, He will provide for you and fill those voids, so you don't have to provide for yourself by participating in sexual activities that war against your soul.

God made us as sexual human beings who have urges. He knows we want to feel important, valuable, and loved by someone special. He made us this way. If God, who made us this way, has the wisdom to design us to have these desires, how much more will He supply our every need in accordance with His riches in glory through Christ Jesus (Philippians 4:19, ESV)?

Go to Him and trust that He will fulfill your every need. Don't try to figure out how He's going to do it, just relinquish all control. Believe that He will do it. Surrender to His plans for you because He knows your life from beginning to end. He created you. Ask Him to fulfill your every need: physical, emotional, financial, relational, spiritual, and mental. He will do it. Watch Him.

I am a person who is in great need of affection. God made me that way, and because He did, I now trust Him to provide that affection for me. This is a legitimate need, and since God created me to need physical touch to feel truly loved, I had confidence that He would provide it. Last year, I visited a family member's church, and apparently, hugging is a part of their culture. It was not until the end of the service when I walked to my car, got in, and closed my door, that I realized how much this church made me feel loved. The affection they gave me was a direct provision from God. He saw my need and attended to it. This is the faithful God I serve, and I am so grateful for His kindness.

Even if we are not able to understand how God is going to provide for our needs does not mean He is not able to do it. We can tell Him the need we have and wait and expect Him to provide. 1 Peter 5:8 (AMP) says, "Casting all your cares [all your anxieties, all your worries, and all your concerns, once and for all] on Him, for He cares about you [with deepest affection, and watches over you very carefully]." *Cast* in the Greek means to throw away, throw off, cast upon, or give up to God (www.blueletterbible.org). Casting care is throwing the concern or needs off of your shoulders and onto God's. He can handle your concerns and fill all of your voids. It is necessary to wait on Him, and I believe that some delays are Divine delays. When we wait on God to provide in His way, we are showing Him that we trust Him. Psalm 27:14 (KJV) says, "Wait on the Lord: be of good courage, and He shall strengthen thine heart: wait, I say, on the Lord."

***

Write down your takeaway from this Step and how you plan to take action:

....

....

....

....

STEP 8

Change Your Environment

Surrounding yourself with people who have achieved what you have set as the desired goal is vital to your freedom from captivity. These should be people who have experienced similar temptations yet overcame them. Someone you can trust not to broadcast all of your struggles and will serve as a person who can empathize with the adjustments you must make to be released from the entanglement of sin.

I remember when I re-dedicated my life to Christ for the fifth or so time. A friend who knew I was desperately in need of a job hired me in a position I was not qualified for. She gave me a chance, and it was a shot in the dark for her but ended up being a blessing in more ways than one for me. I learned a new skill, and I grew in my relationship with the Lord.

She and I developed a stronger friendship as we worked together, and she became a spiritual mentor to me. Being around her every day was one of the things that encouraged and empowered me to change my way of thinking. She introduced me to various genres of Christian music that mirrored my taste in secular music, and I confided in her as she became my accountability and prayer partner.

She was one person in my life who could ask me the hard questions, and I trusted that I was safe with her and could tell her anything. Feeling safe was important for the rebukes that would come when I got off track. God used her mightily in my life, and although we were friends before, this season in our lives bonded us closer together. She is one of my eternal friends that I often thank God for even though we now live miles away from each other. This is a testimony of how God filled a void without me knowing exactly what I needed. He is Jehovah Jireh, the One who sees my needs and provides for every one of them.

This change of environment and having a strong godly support system was the thing that broke me from bad habits. God placed more godly people around me who not only talked like they were Christians but lived as believers even through life's struggles. God blessed me with the opportunity to have a front-row seat in their lives. As a result, I matured tremendously in faith, and I am grateful.

That said, if you are single and trying to stop having sex, it is important for you to change your environment, especially if you and your sexual partner are not on the same page with the decision. You need to tell a trusted godly mentor of your plan to refrain from sex until marriage, so they can pray you through and offer godly wisdom. Also, having a life coach or mentor walk alongside you in this journey will help provide the necessary strength to commit to the change. Lastly, surround yourself with a community of single and married women who have learned from past mistakes and made deliberate decisions to change their lifestyle. Join the Stepping Into Purity and Beyond Group on Facebook to learn more from these women about becoming whole and freed from the bondage of sin.

We often make the mistake of thinking we can stop a bad habit cold turkey in our own power. This is a lie from the enemy. Sexual immorality is a sin against your own body, so it is going to require an intentional, strategic plan to stop.

"Run from sexual sin! No other sin so clearly affects the body as this one does. For sexual immorality is a sin against your own body" (1 Corinthians 6:18 NLT). The word *run* demands that a person departs, separates themselves, takes action, and gets away fast. God designed the physical body to create a strong unbreakable bond through sexual intercourse. In our own power, we do not have the strength to break the alliances we have made with someone sexually. It is impossible to do without God.

Breaking Soul Ties

Serra's Story

Serra had to change her lifestyle. As a young person and a Christian, she was taught at an early age that sex was for married people. She often felt guilty while having sex because she knew it was not God's best for her. However, she would find herself giving in to another sexual encounter only to experience more heartbreak down the road. She felt empty, abandoned, and unloved.

Serra was frustrated because her first committed relationship did not end up in marriage, and some men she got involved with were not interested in anything permanent. Tired of this unfulfilled lifestyle, she made up her mind to let go of this bad habit. Finally, serious about honoring God with her body, she re-dedicated her life to the Lord and made a commitment to herself and to Him that she would not have sex again before marriage.

A little over a year later, Serra got into a committed relationship. She was honest with Mark about her past struggles and told him she would not be participating in premarital sex. He seemed to understand. Serra admired Mark for agreeing to set limits so they would not cross physical boundaries, but there were times when they hung out in his apartment alone, the mood set with low lighting, candles, and romantic music playing. They would hug, kiss, and sometimes end up on his bed entangled in each other's arms. Serra felt safe with Mark but guilty that she was riding the line of physical boundaries with a man when she said she would not have sex again. She was perplexed. Mark seemed to understand what she desired, yet He enjoyed the closeness.

Serra would leave his apartment and drive home with demeaning thoughts going through her mind. She knew she was wrong and was very clear that she was close to breaking her promise again. She was afraid. After all the Lord had done for her, how dare she fall into sexual sin again. What should she do? What did he think about her? Did he think she was weak and unfaithful? Serra was disappointed in herself. How was she going to live a sexually pure lifestyle until marriage? How long would she have to wait to have sex again when getting married seemed farfetched? What if Mark didn't want to wait, or was he agreeing to it because it was important to her? Should she remind him of their conversation? Would he get mad and not want her? She had a lot to think through, and she did not want to lose him.

Serra had reached the point in her life that she would depend on the Lord to break her from this unhealthy habit instead of trying to stop in her own power. When Serra and Mark honored the purity commitment, she felt at peace. However, when they crossed the line, kissing, rolling across his bed bumping and grinding, her heart filled with shame and guilt. Although they never had sex, Serra would drive home disappointed in herself again. Her mind was not pure and going this far filled her heart with guilt. She wished she was stronger.

She entered the door of her house, fell on her knees, and wept bitterly, asking the Lord to forgive her for crossing the line again. She shared with Him all that she desired for her life. Her goal was to be an example of a godly single woman who would honor God by remaining sexually pure in her mind and body before marriage. Serra desired to walk in victory and freedom from sexual sin. She truly wanted to honor herself and the Lord with her whole heart, body, and soul. But in the heat of the moment, she had trouble speaking up for herself.

Each time she found herself breaking her promise again, she expressed this to the Lord in tears. She finally came to the point where she felt safe expressing her thoughts and feelings to the Lord and depending on Him to help her walk in victory. That's when it happened. Mark got a job in another state, and Serra was released from the temptation. Several months later, they broke up. Now, she could recover and go through the process of breaking soul ties.

Maybe you have done everything except sexual intercourse like Serra and Mark or maybe you already went all the way. Understand this. Because sexual encounters are so powerful, ceasing this behavior is going to take accountability, time, and an honest commitment to disengage not only from the act but from anything that exacerbates the situation.

1. To start, disengage with the person you are having sex with. If you are planning to marry him, this does not *necessarily* mean you have to call off the wedding, but you will need to separate from the temptation immediately. Take some time to write down what you plan to say in this conversation so you will be prepared: ....
....
....
....
....

2. Next, pray over yourself, repent, and have a spiritual mentor pray over you to help you break the soul ties that have been formed in your relationship. You need to do this because you have consummated the relationship as if you two were a married couple. You are now joined to someone physically, spiritually, mentally, emotionally, and relationally who has not promised you a permanent commitment by entering into a marital covenant with you. Write a prayer here: ....
....
....
....
....

You may be thinking, *So what?* This is the point I'm making. You have entered into an unlawful agreement in your mind, body, and soul, and you need to surrender to God, admit that your lifestyle has been wrong, ask God for forgiveness, and ask Him to release you from that agreement. You will see in the story below that Susie saw the importance of breaking soul ties before marrying Tommy.

Susie's Story

Right before Tommy and I got married, we both discussed the seriousness of our commitment to one another, especially in the area of our future intimacy. It was actually Tommy that suggested we go separately before God and pray our spiritual connection back from the partners we had sex with prior to our relationship and to allow God to return the spiritual part of that person back to them. Because God is a God of restoration, we could enter our covenant with pure minds, pure hearts, and pure spirits.

Creating this separation is important because the person you have been intimate with has now become a lethal weapon to your desire to be pure. For now, it is best to end the conversations and visits to enable you to clear your head, recalibrate your thinking, and reset your plan for living pure and single.

I am anticipating that you are serious about changing your life and stepping into a new walk of faith with God, and

I am asking God to break those soul ties that are entangling you and renew your mind to one that is honoring to Him. With the Lord's help, you can do this. He will give you the courage to have the hard conversations with those people in your life that are derailing you. Your physical, mental, emotional, and spiritual health is dependent upon this change.

Now, if you're not quite there yet, and are having a hard time imagining yourself living a life without sexual activity, I get it. Been there, done that; it is a process. But think about it. You are changing your whole thought pattern and behavior. For some people, it takes a while to do this successfully. Not only that, but you are also changing the way your body behaves. You will be telling it to stop when it is trying to blaze the trail at high speed.

All you need is a willing heart, and you can ask God for that. If you can let go and allow God to strengthen you to do His will in this area of your life, you will immediately be on the road to recovery. Peace will follow, and eventually, a depth of joy will fill your soul. It is going to be challenging in the beginning. You may feel sad, lonely, or you may second guess yourself. You may wonder if you made a mistake and fantasize about being back in the arms of a man again but know that God is with you. When you obey Him in this, you will have success. I promise.

I know you can do this. It is possible. Remember, the overall goal is to be freed from a lifestyle that has held you captive. You can do this. I believe in you. I have your back.

More importantly, God has your back, and as my home church pastor would say, "He has your slack." He is with you, and He will help you along the way.

***

Write down your takeaway from this Step and how you plan to take action:

....

....

....

....

STEP 9

The Break-Up

As I mentioned in the last step, separating yourself from temptation is essential to correct your behavior successfully. This means you need to end the relationship or at least pause it. Be sure you have a conversation over the phone with the person before ending the relationship.

As a person of noble character, you want to do this in a way that exemplifies integrity and takes the person's feelings into consideration. After all, you two have built an intimate relationship together and shared a lot of memories. If you've been together longer than six months, more than likely, you've introduced him to your family and friends. You have gone places together and shared inside jokes that only the two of you laugh at and understand. A lot has been invested over time, and it will take time to break away from the thoughts and feelings that will flood your mind and heart.

Spending months and years with someone and then dropping them with no explanation (ghosting) is heartless and can be detrimental to a person's emotional health. Take responsibility for the heart of the person you fell in love with. Be courageous and honest about the reason you are backing off.

If you profess to be a Christian, you have an honorable duty to protect the heart of the man you've been intimate with, especially if he is your brother in Christ. You can start by confessing that you have not lived according to God's standards, and you have been feeling guilty about it. Share your desire to follow Jesus and His standards instead of your own. Share that you have prayed about it, and you are trusting God to strengthen you and allow you to honor the commitment you made to Him to stop having sex while you are single. Tell him you need to break ties with him until further notice to gain momentum in this new commitment to the Lord.

The Bible says premarital sex is a sin (I Corinthians 6:18, NKJV). The sexual relationship between a man and woman should be within the covenant of a husband and wife. This confession allows you to stand on the truth of who God made sex for and acknowledge that you agree with His plan. Saying this aloud is as much for you as it is for the other person. Ask the person for forgiveness and let them know that going forward, you will not be in touch with them.

If you have any important possessions (clothing, keys, pictures, expensive gifts, sacrificial gifts, etc.), give them back or throw them away as an act of letting go and breaking ties with memories of this person. Bathe your conversation in prayer and make sure your communication is clear. Let your yes be yes, and your no be no (Matthew 5:37, NKJV). You do not want to sound tentative. This could cause confusion, and the person may assume the door is not all the way closed. Leave not one crack in that door. Reiterate that the relationship is no longer working for you. At this point, you will no longer be in contact with him, but wish him the very best.

Breathe.

Now write down the thoughts and feelings you are experiencing right now:

....

....

....

....

I know it may hurt just thinking about how this is all going to go, and processing the thought of not talking to him anymore. It breaks my heart to think that you are going through this and probably feeling physical pain in your heart right now. I remember the pain. It is scary, and it hurts, especially if you have found comfort in the security of a man and if your identity as a girlfriend has been extremely meaningful to you. Breathe, beautiful one. Breathe. Although you feel pain right now, you will get through this. Try not to call him for comfort. Call on Jesus. If you can be still and let God do what He does best, this will be a time where you can get to know God the Comforter. He will comfort you. He did it for me, and I know He will do it for you. Rest. Cry, yes, but then take another deep breath and rest some more. He's got you. I promise.

Now you can ask God for forgiveness. Do not be fearful of admitting your wrong to Him. You are safe with Him, I promise. The God of the universe, He who created you, can love you back to life. He can give you a new, adventurous life that you never thought you would live. He will honor your obedience.

One thing that may help you part ways with the person you were dating is to journal your way through the pain. Designate four sheets of paper from your journal. On the first sheet, write down everything you can think of that you enjoyed about the relationship. On the second sheet of paper, write what you did not like about the relationship. On the third sheet, write your dreams and goals even if they are far-fetched. On the last sheet, write your regrets and what you will do differently in the next relationship. In the end, all of this work will be worth the struggle.

You may be wondering what exactly happened after Mark left town.

Serra found the courage to talk with Mark. She noticed that his commitment level was decreasing, and he was not as available as he had been in the past. Sometimes he would go a week or so without calling. It was obvious that other things took priority over their relationship. She needed to break up with him but feared having the conversation. She discussed this with a godly friend who agreed that she needed to end the relationship and gave her some talking points to help her express what she was feeling.

Serra called Mark and said, "Mark, this is not working out for me. I need to take some time to figure out my life and get my priorities in order. I have noticed that our relationship has been greatly affected by our lack of communication. There are times when I have not been able to reach you, and we don't talk as often as we did in the past. Thank you for the years we have spent with each other and for all the memories. I will not forget them. I still love you, but I must make some changes for my emotional and spiritual health."

Serra did not attack Mark with her words because she was hurting, nor did she drive several hours to stalk him and slash his tires. She owned her feelings and desires. She realized that he was not benefitting her anymore, asked for advice before calling, and took responsibility to end the relationship with him. Mark had disconnected emotionally, and she realized that she wanted more than he was willing to give.

Serra recovered by evaluating what happened, talking to God about it, and vowing to change the narrative of her story by correcting her mistakes. Eventually, she broke free from that soul tie. It may seem impossible, but if you apply the truths in this book, you can break free too. Keep reading, my sister.

***

Write down your takeaway from this Step and how you plan to take action:

....

....

....

....

STEP 10

Get a Spiritual Mentor

To stand the test of time, you will need a mentor and accountability partner. This is a person (or people) who is committed to praying for you. They can sense your spiritual gifts and can pray with you so the enemy cannot hinder your purpose from being fulfilled.

Being sexually intimate with a partner will become the undercurrent to your purpose, so you need a spiritual mentor who knows who you are and where you are going. This should be someone who is rich in wisdom and can discern what God is saying and can confirm if what you have heard is correct. They should be a person above reproach who can hold you accountable to all God is calling you to do. The only way this person can discern the voice of God is if they are knowledgeable of God's Word and can appropriately apply scriptures to a given situation. This person is spiritually mature, gives practical application, and is someone you can receive correction from and act on it. To avoid any conflict of interest, they should be of the same gender and someone who operates in integrity.

Write down the names of two or three women you can ask to be your mentor or accountability partner:

....

....

....

Initially, you may want to meet with this person once a week to help you and then space it out to once a month or so to avoid developing an unhealthy dependence on this person. Keep in mind that the Holy Spirit is your teacher, and He will coach you. Your first allegiance is to Him, then let Him point you to a mentor who can help you.

If you don't have a mentor you can physically meet with, you can follow your favorite author or speaker online. In 2016, I began following a few people online who have become virtual mentors to me. I have grown tremendously in confidence, entrepreneurial skills, spiritual maturity, and physical and emotional health. Social media groups, books, videos, blogs, and conferences can also serve as mentoring resources in your life in the areas of need.

Mentors can help give support as strongholds are broken in your life. Through prayer, your mentor can help you break those soul ties that entangle you. In the first thirty days, it will be important to get in touch with them weekly so you can stay focused and on track, and they can get to know you better and pray for you. They can affirm that you did the right things and help ward off the negative things the enemy may say to you as you are trying to go in another direction.

You will also need to cleanse yourself from things that have attached to you through that person by confession, asking for forgiveness, and renouncing any bitterness, resentment, and anger that has not been resolved. Go back to Steps 1-3 to do the exercises again if you need to. As you let go of old things and embrace the new, you will need all of these reinforcements to be successful. The right mentor can help with this.

***

Write down your takeaway from this Step and how you plan to take action:

....

....

....

....

Study, Recite and Memorize God's Word

Studying, reciting aloud, and memorizing God's Word will give you the power you need to break free from premarital sex. The Bible will equip you with the truth you need to develop, strengthen, and reinforce the confidence you will gain to continue this journey of abstinence.

First, you need to know what God says about you in His Word. John 3:16 (NIV) says, "For God so loved the world that He gave His one and Son, that whosoever believes in Him shall not perish but have eternal life." He loved you so much that He gave His most precious possession so that you can have a permanent relationship with Him. He provided a way for you to escape eternal separation from Him. He has a plan and purpose in mind for you, to prosper you, not to harm you; a plan for a hope and a bright future (Jeremiah 29:11, NIV). Always remember that God loves you with an everlasting love. With unfailing love, He drew you to Himself (Jeremiah 31:3, NLT), and such love has no fear because perfect love expels all fear (I John 4:18, NLT). If we are afraid, it is for fear of punishment, and this shows that we have not fully experienced his perfect love (1 John 4:18, NLT).

Whatever you need, God will supply it according to His riches in glory in Christ Jesus (Philippians 4:19, ESV). If you need power and strength to resist temptation, He will provide this for you. So, don't be afraid, because He is with you; don't be anxious, because He is your God. He will strengthen you and help you. He will uphold you with His victorious right hand (Isaiah 41:10, ISV). So be strong and courageous. Do not be afraid, and do not panic. For the LORD, your God will personally go ahead of you. He will neither fail you nor abandon you (Deuteronomy 31:6, NLT).

These scriptures are some of my favorite Bible verses that have empowered me and gotten me through hard times over the years. What are some of your favorite scriptures that have sustained and strengthened you? ....

....

....

Remember that God's Word proves to you that He is on your side. Follow His lead and know that He will not leave you alone to figure out how to live pure.

It's imperative to know what the scripture says about sexual sin. This truth will allow you to identify the lies that you have believed. These lies have infiltrated your mind and deceived you into thinking it is truth. Knowing and memorizing the scriptures is one of the most powerful tools you can use to ultimately destroy your flesh and keep you focused on righteous living. Applying God's Word to your life will strengthen your spirit and weaken your flesh. Your flesh will no longer have the power it has been using to assault you and, in turn, will give you the power to ward off evil spirits, allowing you to grow in the nurturing grace and admonition of the Lord.

Here are some scriptures that speak about God's heart towards sex outside of marriage:

1 Corinthians 6:18 NLT- "Run from sexual sin! No other sin so clearly affects the body as this one does. For sexual immorality is a sin against your own body."

Ephesians 5:3 NIV- "But among you, there must not be even a hint of sexual immorality, or of any kind of impurity, or of greed, because these are improper for God's holy people."

Galatians 5:19a NLT- "When you follow the desires of your sinful nature, the results are very clear: sexual immorality, impurity, lustful pleasures..."

1 Thessalonians 4:3-5 (NLT) - "God's will is for you to be holy, so stay away from all sexual sin. Then each of you will control his own body and live in holiness and honor—not in lustful passion like the pagans who do not know God and his ways."

What other scriptures come to mind? ....

....

....

Most single people who have delved into sexual sin have been deceived into thinking they will gain something by continuing this behavior. But this thinking begs the question: What have you gained from this intimate relationship? Have you gained peace, security, and loyalty, or have you gained temporary comfort, worry, and heartbreak?

An example of a lie from the enemy is that you are loved and valued when you have sex with a man, and if this man is not in your life, you are not worth anything. But the truth is the perfect love of God sends fear far away from you. Believing this gets rid of all false indications that you are nothing without a man. I am here to tell you that you are everything God intended for you to be, whether the fullness of this is present or not.

My friend, love did not come from having sex with a man. God is Love and Love is God. Love comes from knowing and believing that God saw you first. He formed and fashioned you just like you are, and He has been pursuing you ever since you were born. Psalm 139:13-16 (TLB) says, "You made all the delicate, inner parts of my body and knit them together in my mother's womb. Thank you for making me so wonderfully complex! It is amazing to think about.

Your workmanship is marvelous—and how well I know it. You were there while I was being formed in utter seclusion! You saw me before I was born and scheduled each day of my life before I began to breathe. Every day was recorded in your book!"

God holds you in high value. He knows and wants the very best for you. He wants you to experience His love and not some fabricated love that has been derived by the media. He has surrounded you with people who love you and admire you.

Here's an assignment for you. It may take some guts to do it but ask the closest people around you why they love you and what they admire about you. If this does not fill up your love tank, I don't know what will. Don't be embarrassed to ask. Tell them you are working on recognizing your own value and wanted to know their opinion. Even more than asking your loved ones, ask yourself.

Get your pen and journal. Go to a quiet space where you can think. Divide the page into four columns and write these questions at the top of each column:

1) What do I love and admire about ME? ....

2) What do I do well? ....

3) What are my strengths? ....

4) What compliments have I heard people give me? ......
....

This exercise will not make you conceited. It will make you appreciate how God designed you.

God's arms are always open wide for you to come to Him. He is the one who truly values you. He declared your worth long ago. The absence of a person in your life does not subtract from your worth. Your worth was already determined from the beginning.

Let's get rid of all deceptions that have been sent to derail our value. Find a quiet place and take at least thirty minutes to renounce all beliefs from the enemy and all alliances you have made with him. We are going to replace those ungodly beliefs with the truth of God's Word.

- I renounce the lie that I am only valuable when I have the love of a man.

- I renounce the lie that I am not worth anything unless I have a man in my life.

- I renounce the lie that I am less than others because I do not have a significant other in my life.

- I renounce the lie that my life is worthless unless I am dating, married, and/or have children.

- I renounce the lie that my life is boring because I am not dating.

- I renounce the lie that I am not loved because I do not have a husband.

- I renounce the lie that I am alone because I am not involved in a relationship.

Your turn:

- I renounce ....
- I renounce ....
- I renounce ....
- I believe and accept the truth that God loves me so much that He gave His only begotten Son to take on my punishment and die for me so I could experience freedom.

- I believe and accept the truth that the God of the universe wants an intimate relationship with me.

- I believe and accept the truth that my worth and value are not determined by who is in my life.

- I believe and accept the truth that God holds me in the palm of His hand and will not allow anyone to pluck me out.

- I believe and accept the truth that no weapon formed against me shall prosper, and I will condemn the enemy who rises against me to accuse me of being worthless or further reinforce the lie that I am not valuable because a man does not love me.

- I believe and accept the truth that I am the apple of God's eye.

- I believe and accept the truth that God knows who is best for me and will provide people who love me unconditionally.

Your turn:

- I believe and accept ....
....

- I believe and accept ....
....

- I believe and accept ....
....

We must memorize scripture so we can stay focused and use them for combat when the enemy comes in like a flood and tries to tempt us to return to our old pattern of thinking. We know temptation will come. The Bible speaks about this in 1 Corinthians 10:13 (TLB), "But remember this—the wrong desires that come into our life aren't anything new. Many others have faced exactly the same problems before you. And no temptation is irresistible. You can trust God to keep the temptation from becoming so strong that you can't stand up against it, for He has promised this and will do what He says. He will show you how to escape temptation's power so that you can bear up patiently against it."

Exercising self-control and patience are critical to maintaining a sexually pure lifestyle. Knowing God and the scriptures will empower you to successfully live this out. God's Word gives you direction when you are going to be tempted.

***

Write down your takeaway from this Step and how you plan to take action:

....

....

....

....

Speak Out Words of Declaration

Now that you know God's Word, your worth, and recognize your admirable qualities, you have to declare that with your mouth every day. You have been depleting your value by allowing someone who has not entered into a covenant with you to have access to your most prized possessions. As I said earlier, when you have premarital sex, you are entrusting your mind, body, and soul to someone who has not committed themselves to you. I heard someone say this years ago. When we have sex with someone who is not our spouse, we are committing future children to this person. This could create unwanted drama for your child. Think forward and avoid this by infusing yourself with truth and resetting your mind to what God originally said about you. What He says about you is absolutely true. It can never be changed. He created you to be able to fulfill His plan. And His plan is always better than we can imagine.

Luke 10:27 (NIV) reminds us to "love the Lord your God with all of your heart and with all your soul and with all your strength and with all your mind." The second part of that verse is to "love your neighbor as yourself." Most people would say it is selfish to love yourself, or if you love yourself too much, you will become conceited. However, you are not able to love people if you do not love God first and love yourself.

Loving God can be done by spending time with Him in worship, talking to Him, depending on Him, listening to Him, and doing what He says. Loving yourself is honoring God because He created you, and He made no mistakes in designing you just the way you are. Psalm 139:14 (ESV) says, "you are fearfully and wonderfully made." The author confidently declares that the Lord's works are extraordinarily breathtaking!

Guard Your Heart

God has a love for you that is contagious. You have to love yourself to honor Him. As you love and invest in yourself and guard the heart He gave you, you will have the potential to make wiser decisions in your relationships. In doing this, you will find that the negative inner chatter that goes on inside your head will cease. When the faulty thinking stops, affirmations can take root and grow into higher godly self-esteem and self-confidence, and this will change everything.

Several times I have had to make the hard decision to guard my heart so it would not be ensnared by the enemy. I remember my first time away from my hometown. I moved to a city three hours north, and I went through so much in making the final decision to move. There was excitement, tears, packing, putting my house on the market, and so much more for me to consider. I was happy yet a little concerned. I felt supported yet lonely. This area was my heart's desire. I had wanted to move for six years, but it did not happen in my timing. The Lord had to add a bit more skill to my life that was going to prepare me for this change. I waited, He promoted me, and then finally, the moment came. It was timely but still a surprise, to say the least.

I felt like I was in a whole new world. Although I moved within the same state, the city I moved to was totally different from where I grew up. Everything was new: the culture, the roadways, the traffic, the people, and their lifestyles. Everything. I moved in temporarily with someone kind enough to let me rent a room until I found a permanent place to stay. I was thankful but apprehensive.

I was not in my new temporary place a week before I received an inquiry from a man in my inbox. This was someone I had never had a private conversation with before that day. He told me he had a family member who lived in my new city and asked if he could visit. My interest was piqued, but I declined to accept his visit after finding out he was in the middle of a divorce. Why now? Why, after not having any interaction with a male for five years, would someone who was not fully available reach out to me? I considered keeping in contact with the man, but a few things happened that left me feeling suspicious and uncomfortable.

Right after that came to an end, another man hit me up in my inbox. *What in the world is going on here?* One after another. I had not gotten this much attention since I was out living like someone in the world. This second man lived within an hour's drive, and he was very engaging. He seemed interested in the things I was interested in, and he was sincerely trying to get to know me better. He was intelligent and pursuing the things of God. He was tall, handsome, genuine, fun to talk to, and asked good questions.

I knew him from the area I grew up in and had always admired him. He was a deep thinker, and I liked that. He had a great memory and recalled several interactions we had. I was intrigued. I could see a relationship developing down the road with this man, but I was guarding my heart and chose not to give a lot in our conversations. Careful not to dive in and share all of my thoughts and desires, I cautiously kept the door of communication open, trying not to reveal that I was guarded. As we got to know each other, I found out that he, too, was in the middle of a divorce and did not have a definite date when things would be finalized. I let that go too. I declined his invitation to go out on a date because I wanted to make sure he was completely out of that chapter of his life before attempting to start another with me.

Lesson learned, ladies. A man who is "separated" is still married. As a counselor, I was concerned about both men. They were newly separated and needed time alone to allow God to heal their hearts and renew their minds. If not, there was a possibility that they would drag their past baggage into a relationship with me. The healing process, after being in a marriage with someone, is important. It takes time, and I knew that. It was tempting to let things happen and not think it through, but praise God, I was able to make a good choice to walk away from both situations without getting entangled in another situation where I would create more regrets.

It was not easy, and I was lonely. The men who reached out to me were filling a void I had, but I could not let that dominate me. I had to look past where I was at the moment and discern what I wanted in the future. I decided that I wanted a man who was totally available.

I told both men I would no longer be continuing conversations with them. I felt it was important to have this conversation and not just drop off the face of the earth like some people often do. The most important decision here stemmed from me not wanting to violate the promise I made to myself before the Lord years after making so many unwise choices. I don't think the men understood where I was coming from, and I chose not to go into a lot of detail because I wanted to be careful that I would not be talked out of my decision to cut off all communication. God was gracious; neither man put up a fight and respectfully let me go.

The situation above is an example of guarding your heart. Protecting your heart means you have to know who you are in the Lord. Sometimes you will have to make some hard decisions, but this will certainly build up your confidence by recognizing that you can resist the good to get the best. You will feel better about yourself when you set boundaries that serve as a protection for the bright future you have ahead.

Now let's take some time to reflect. Have you ever gotten emotionally consumed when getting to know a man? Have you been entangled with someone you never thought you would get involved with? I don't think I am by myself here. It happens. So, take some time to reflect. Track your steps, write down how it happened, and consider what you could have done differently?

....
....
....
....
....

As time went on, I had to learn from my past mistakes to prevent my heart and mind from getting consumed with a person again. While taking time off from dating, I learned that my heart is tender, and I am prone to get entangled prematurely. I know the enemy wanted me to get caught up in a relationship that was not right before the Lord. I learned to set boundaries with myself beforehand and abide by them in dating relationships so that I could live in peace within myself and before the Lord.

You guard your heart by not entertaining people, and conversations that you know will cause you to become too emotionally vested. You have to make sure that you are not entering into a situation that will cause you to become entangled in sin, with no hope of being free apart from the power of God coming through on your behalf.

John 10:10 (ESV) says, "The thief comes only to steal, kill, and destroy. I came that they may have life and have it abundantly." The negative inner chatter will be temporary, but the negativity cannot stay when you know the truth about what God says about you and declare it out loud. All thoughts, accusations, and negativity have to go, and believe me, it will.

Knowing and experiencing the abundant life God has planned will launch you into a place in your life where the love for yourself will overflow into the lives of those around you. You will become more pleasant to be around and will attract positive, like-minded people in your life. People will recognize that you are making life choices that add value and will want to know more about the joy and peace you possess. Your relationship with God and others will increase the likelihood of you choosing healthy relationships where you can learn new things, mature, and be encouraged to accomplish all the things God has for you to achieve. This positive life change can also put you in a position to recognize the man God has for you. Notice that I did not say "find the man God has for you." I said, recognize him. When you have a more hope-filled outlook on life, it tends to change the lenses in which you see everything in life. Shifting your focus will change the entire trajectory of your life.

* * *

Write down your takeaway from this Step and how you plan to take action:

....

....

....

....

STEP 13

Join a Bible-teaching, Christ-centered Church

A spiritual covering, as in a church, is needed so you can continue to mature in the faith, be accountable to a group of people, and be cared for in your spiritual journey. Developing a relationship with a smaller group of like-minded people within your church will be an important step to your success in living a transformed life. These are people who are followers of Jesus through relationship, word, thought, and deed. The way you can determine this is by observing the way they live and respond to the teaching of God's Word outside the public eye.

If you are not currently a member of a body of believers, look for a Bible-believing, teaching church whose pastor is a man of integrity, and whose members have a personal relationship with the Lord and follow the teaching of God's Word. What vital characteristics do you need in a church to ignite your spiritual growth? ....

....

....

A few years ago, when moving from my hometown. I knew I needed to look for a church that had a pastor who believed and taught from the Bible as well as urged the members to live according to biblical standards. This was important to me because I was raised in this type of church. I went to a church service, a book study, and a small group for singles. Throughout all of these activities and side conversations with members, I saw a consistent theme of integrity in real authentic Christ-centered living. As I could tell, these people were not legalistic, superficial, or unfaithful to the Lord. I attended and participated in activities for months before joining to make sure I was making the right decision, and these pleasant discoveries moved me to join that church. I truly believe God sent me down that road, led my eyes to the sign, and whispered in my heart, "visit this church."

Surround yourself with believers of Jesus Christ who will be instrumental in teaching you and equipping you with what the word of the Lord says. Join a place of worship where you can ask questions, attend Bible studies and learn more about how Christians live a godly life in this world full of wickedness and strife. 2 Corinthians 5:17 (HCSB) says, "Therefore, if anyone is in Christ, He is a new creation; old things have passed away, and look, new things have come." Since you are no longer living your old lifestyle, you will need some direction on what the new should look like.

Being connected with members of the body of Christ will ensure that you are cared for, checked on, and poured into regularly. Galatians 6:10 (NLT) says, "Therefore, whenever we have the opportunity, we should do good to everyone—especially to those in the family of faith." We in God's family should be committed to protecting each other and walking alongside one another for fellowship and in times of need.

Being a part of a church body will allow you to identify the spiritual gifts God has given you upon becoming a believer. You will discover areas where you can volunteer according to your knowledge, gifts, and strengths. It is also a place where you can give back to the Lord financially to invest in His kingdom and see the lives of people changed.

***

Write down your takeaway from this Step and how you plan to take action:

....

....

....

....

....

STEP 14

Choose God's Best

God wants you to live your best life according to all the things that He planned for you before the foundations of the world were laid. I am certain that He does not want the counterfeit things that you have pursued on your own. This life that you are living has to be rooted in your decision to trust a faithful God who has more for you than you can think or even imagine. He can do exceedingly and abundantly above all your heart desires.

It is your choice, though. God, in His infinite wisdom, humility, and vulnerability, has given you the luxury of choosing what you are going to do. He does not force us to go His way. He lays out the plan for us in His Word, and through the Holy Spirit's divine revelation, He says, "Choose this day whom you will serve" (Joshua 24:15a, ESV). This is a direct manifestation of the Lord's kindness towards us. He will not force His way into our lives. He knows once we commit to being in fellowship with Him, our relationship with Him will be more intimate and enjoyable.

Thrive During the Wait

The Hebrew meaning of wait is *qavah*, which means to wait, look eagerly for, hope, expect.

Another part of this definition is to collect or bind together, perhaps by twisting into a rope. When we are waiting with the Lord on His plan to develop our lives, we are waiting collectively with and on Him, and we are waiting alongside many other single people who have committed to saving themselves for marriage. God will not let you go. He is in it with you. Yes, He does know how you feel because He created you to desire a relationship with the opposite sex. Don't ever doubt that. I am not encouraging you to walk around in denial of the fact that you are a sexual being who needs intimacy. However, God's plan is for you to enjoy sex with your husband. What has been your response to waiting on God for a spouse?

Ladies, to be honest, I have felt frustrated sometimes and other times, I have been content. What I am imploring you to do is to try God's way. Test Him. Let Him prove to you that He can free you and launch you into a lifestyle that you have never imagined living. It can happen. There is a way to date that honors the Lord. With your commitment to listen to God, use wisdom, and seek the support of praying mentors, you will see this change happen right in front of your eyes.

Here is an example of a godly woman who dated wisely, waited for the one who captured all of her heart, and avoided the snare of sexual sin. It took patience, commitment, wisdom, and self-determination. There is no doubt that Michelle's love story was written by the hand of God. She knew her goals and aspirations and committed to them. She was passionate about the dreams that were on her heart, and she was determined to wait to get the results she wanted - a pure intimate marital relationship with a man whose goals and dreams aligned with hers.

Michelle's Story

I chose to be celibate before marriage. My upbringing as a Christian and the biblical principles I learned as a child influenced this decision. As I grew into my teen and college years, I learned about the social-emotional health and wellness benefits of my choice as well as the wisdom, freedom, and increased sound judgment that grows with each interaction without the pressure or commitment of a sexual relationship.

As a teen and young adult, this abstinent lifestyle provided me with the freedom to enjoy multiple career-building opportunities, develop leadership skills, and enhance many friendships to make prudent choices when I was ready because I wasn't distracted by relationships or tied down to conflicted feelings related to being intimate. I was preoccupied with many leadership roles in graduate school, the workplace, and the ministries I had started. I didn't regularly spend a lot of time with men because I was heavily involved with mentoring women. I was pretty driven and wanted to excel in my craft.

I also realize that I didn't have many girlfriends who were preoccupied with romantic relationships. I observed the marriages of my older sisters and knew the right guy would come along in due time. Maybe I worried my parents a bit in my early twenties because I was not "looking for love," but being upfront about personal boundaries narrowed the relationship field to those who were equally committed to respecting my space and values.

In my friendships with men, my approach was one of gathering information before exploring intimate feelings. I enjoyed having F.B.I. dialogues, learning about his family, experiences, and cultural dynamics. I explored their belief systems regarding faith and morality. I wanted to learn about their interest in changing the world, their vision, dreams, prayers, future, career, and community impact.

I faced a few experiences of rejection because some men didn't possess the same standards I held. Some thought I was playing "hard to get" and realized quickly that it wasn't a game but a focus and commitment. Others enjoyed the friendship yet chose to move on out of respect for my choices. But the difficulty was always temporary as I realized that the right person at the right time would be worth the work.

Before meeting my husband, I was involved in mostly casual friendships, and the few relationships that tried to move in a romantic direction were either halted due to other priorities or long distance. I had a positive experience with my college boyfriend, but by my senior year, that relationship stalled due to spiritual differences. Because I knew I had a specific calling of leadership on my life, I was sensitive to the Holy Spirit's prompting.

After college, I remember being interested in a guy, and although the feelings were mutual, after visiting me, he stated that I would be well respected on his campus because of my standards, but he only wanted a friendship with me at that time. Surprisingly, I wasn't hurt by his reaction because I had sincerely prayed for the direction of the relationship and protection over my heart. I remember asking God to give me peace with the outcome of the visit. It may sound crazy, but I was expectant and quite relieved. I thanked him for his honesty and wished him well in his life. I also felt physically and emotionally free because we hadn't kissed or had any inappropriate embraces that I had wasted or would regret. We ended the friendship, and a few months later, my husband-to-be and I connected and began a friendship.

When I met my husband-to-be, his character was attractive to me. I chose to date him because I first observed his authentic engagement with people of all backgrounds and his commitment to his faith. I later enjoyed his interactions with me and his curiosity about my life and future goals. He was different from everyone else. He stood out from the crowd, and with a lot of thought and input from wise counsel, we decided to get to know each other better.

We were long distanced during our friendship and courtship. It was a year and a half from the time we met to the time we married. The long-distance allowed our affection to be displayed through words. Since we both committed to not kissing one another, I felt less pressure to engage physically when we were together. Although, the closer we got to the wedding date, and the more time we spent in the same city, the deeper my affection grew for him in ways that I hadn't experienced with other men. The more we got to know each other in a long-distance friendship, the more his walk and talk aligned with mine.

We each had many accountability partners who connected with us during and after our visits as well as many gatherings with groups to prevent too much alone time, especially in the evenings. We also had mentors and friends in common and were able to receive insight from them as well. We would remind each other that

June (our wedding month) was coming soon, and we couldn't wait to express ourselves physically. His commitment to similar standards of intimacy throughout our friendship also pointed to his character and freed us to pursue matters of the heart.

The freedom I enjoyed as a single woman in friendships, excluding intimate relations, allowed me to fully engage intimately with my husband, and it was so much fun! And seventeen years later, it still is!

I encourage all single women to trust your values. Honor God and your faith. Love yourself. Allow your mind and heart to take time to connect fully and authentically. Continue to seek out great mentors and friends who respect your standards. You can do this!

I trust that you were able to glean some insights and wisdom from Michelle's story. I sure did. We can all learn from her experience which challenges us to pursue our purpose while we are single, take the time to get to know the person of interest to see if our values align, resist temptation, and wait patiently on God to provide for our needs. Maybe you did not do it this way the first time for whatever reason. Like me, you may have missed the mark several times but here's the good news. We all have the opportunity to restart. All of us have the freedom to try again and experience the desired change empowered by the grace of God.

Write down your takeaway from this Step and how you plan to take action:

....

....

....

....

....

....

....

....

Let Freedom Ring

Whose you go through these steps, you are going to have the freedom to walk in newness of life. As a new creation, old things are in the past. It's a new day! You can look forward to new and exciting things happening in your life. The enlightenment, along with the achievements you are about to make, will give you the confidence and security you have always needed when making decisions in your relationships.

The whole purpose of this book is to challenge you to approach this new path of purity and freedom with courage. You will make mistakes and may experience a setback or two, but every day is a day you can start over again. As you commit yourself to the Lord, you will break this cycle and live victoriously. With the Lord's help and many people's prayers, I did it, and I know you can.

The Bible says all other sins a person commits are outside the body, but whoever sins sexually, sins against their own body (1 Corinthians 6:18b, NIV). You have to break this cycle and keep it broken. When you break this cycle, you will have the courage, confidence, and strength to break other cycles in your life with the Lord's help.

This freedom will grant you peace with Almighty God so that you are not always looking over your shoulder and judging every problem that arises in your life as punishment from Him. This kind of thinking is certainly not the will of the Lord. The devil comes only to steal, kill, and destroy, but Jesus came that we may have life abundantly (John 10:10, NKJV). Your life should be a wonderful secure adventure with the faithful God of the universe.

Living apart from God's will makes you anxious and paranoid. You will worry if the guy is faithful, wonder if that itch is a sexually transmitted disease, and become concerned about being pregnant. Then, if you become pregnant, you may be tempted to abort the baby in an effort to keep your wayward lifestyle hidden. The bottom line is that living outside of God's will induces misery. You may experience pleasure for a season, but trust me, it will only be temporary. It's just not worth it.

Seeking freedom in your new lifestyle with Christ will be rewarding. Hebrews 11:6b (NKJV) says, God rewards those who diligently seek Him. You cannot get a better deal than that. My encouragement to you is to do all you can to get on this freedom path. If you want it, you can have the peace of God right now. Seek God for your freedom. Seek Him wholeheartedly, and you will find Him (Jeremiah 29:13, NLT).

If you have done the exercises in this book — confessed your sins to God, asked for forgiveness, shared it with a spiritually mature friend, and changed your environment — you are off to a great start. Change is hard, but when you make up your mind to do it, you will realize that this place is where you can reposition yourself and redirect your steps so that you can recalibrate. Remember to get into God's Word. Memorize and declare His promises to you and learn His expectations of you. Identify any self-defeating lies you've made alliances with, break them, and replace those deceptions from satan with the Word of God. Declare your worth out loud so you and the enemy can hear it. Repeat this every day, and I promise you will experience the freedom of God like never before. As a result, you will become instrumental in setting the captives free and releasing prisoners around you who are struggling with the same thing.

Be committed to following these steps. Be aware that the devil will come back and make you think that all of this work you have done to be free was in vain and that it never happened. I am telling you, my friend, that you are F-R-E-E. This is what God says about you, and I agree with Him. John 8:36 (NKJV) says, "Therefore if the Son makes you free, you shall be free indeed."

What changes do you need to make in your life to experience the freedom Christ came to give you? ....
....
....

Do not believe the hype of the enemy. He comes to steal your freedom and ultimately destroy you. He will lie to you. His job is to deceive you into thinking you are not strong enough to sustain this change in your life, and he is right about that. You are not strong enough to do it in your own power, but with the power of the blood of Jesus, you are set free, and God will sustain you so that you can remain free as long as you want it for yourself. Sister, agree with me that you are free. Say it out loud. Yes! I hear you, girl. You sure are. Before the Lord, and by the power He put in me, I declare you to be free in the name of Jesus Christ.

Now it's your turn.

Proclaim it out loud.

"I am free, indeed!"

Let Freedom Ring in Heaven!

Let Freedom Ring in all the Earth!

Let Freedom Ring in my soul!

Let Freedom Ring in my heart!

Let Freedom Ring in my mind!

Let Freedom Ring in my body!

Let Freedom Ring around my home!

Let Freedom Ring in my ears!

Let Freedom Ring from my mouth!

Let Freedom Ring in every footstep I take!

Let Freedom Ring in my gifting!

Let Freedom Ring in my purpose!

Let Freedom Ring in my job!

Let Freedom Ring in my church!

Let Freedom Ring in my relationships!

Let Freedom Ring in my family!

Let Freedom Ring in my children!

Let Freedom Ring in my legacy!

Let Freedom Ring, Let Freedom Ring, Let Freedom Ring!

***

Write down your takeaway from this Step and how you plan to take action:

....

....

....

....

....

WHERE DO WE GO FROM HERE?

Once God sets you free and allows you to walk out of captivity and into purity, you must maintain your healing. You will not be able to sit back, relax, and do nothing. You must be careful to do what it says in 1 Peter 5:8 (NLT), "Stay alert! Watch out for your great enemy, the devil. He prowls around like a roaring lion, looking for someone to devour." The enemy does not want you to be free. He wants you to get tripped up again. He ultimately wants to destroy you and will do all he can to make sure you are ineffective and miserable if he is not able to destroy you.

This life of freedom will require you to make some changes. There are things that you will have to put aside to stay pure in your mind, body, and spirit.

Mind

When we change our lifestyle to one that is pure, holy, and acceptable to God, we have to put to death fantasies and memories in our minds. We have to literally go to war against every scheme the devil will throw our way. Images that we have seen will pop up at the most inopportune time. You will have to put some things into action to eliminate the temptation that will come your way.

There are times when I have to turn my head, plug my ears, switch the station, change the channel, leave the room, press mute, or press stop on a movie or song. I avoid anything that could take me places in my head that I don't need to go. It's amazing how it can happen so fast.

There have been times in my life when I've been at church, and suddenly, unpleasant thoughts come into my mind. I don't understand how it happens, but I attribute those times to memories from the past and onslaughts straight from the enemy. At that moment, I have the choice to give in to temptation and entertain those vain imaginations or pray God's Word out loud over my mind. For example, an image will come my way, and I will say, "Lord, I thank you that I have the mind of Christ. I rebuke that thought in the mighty name of Jesus. It is not from You, and I replace it with the truth that I have a pure mind, and I am a forgiven holy woman who desires to please you in everything I do and say."

Body

Attacks within your body can be a trigger, particularly if you have committed to be pure and save any type of sexual activity until marriage. You will miss being held, penetrated, made to feel special, valued, and desired. Your body will go through withdrawals because it is accustomed to receiving attention sexually, which will now be inactive. Allow yourself to adjust to the change. Challenge yourself not to go back and restart the cycle you just worked hard to break.

As your body goes through the detoxification process:

1. Ask for God's grace to strengthen you.

2. Trust that He will surely see you through.

3. Start a workout plan to help relieve your body of stress.

4. Cease any activities, music, or movies that turn your body's SEX NOW light on.

5. Stop talking about it so much. Sometimes the more we talk about it, the more power you give it.

6. Avoid being in tempting situations with men. Create boundaries that you will not cross and keep your accountability partner or mentor informed on how you are doing with this.

Your turn: Is there anything else you need to do to successfully go through the detoxification process? If so, write it here.

....

....

....

....

When you do the work, day after day, week after week, month after month, you will gain momentum in remaining sexually pure by the power of God, our Father. The Holy Spirit is our guide, teacher, and our comforter. Trust that His power will enable you to maintain the commitment you've made. Talk to God when you want to give in to the urges. Tell Him that your body is screaming for fellowship, if you know what I mean. Although God will never suggest that you sin to put out this fire, when you ask, He will put it on ice and gift you with the grace to live an abundant life that pleases Him.

Spirit

Most likely, satan will tell you that you will fail miserably, you don't have what it takes, there is no way this is going to work, no one lives like this, no one will want you if you make this commitment to purity, and you will never get married. Satan is a big fat liar. You can do this. If I can do it, you surely can do it.

You have to trust the voice of the Lord that tells you to run from sexual sin (1 Corinthians 6:18, NIV). God would never say something that He doesn't mean. He would never ask you to run from something good. He wants the very best for your life. Psalm 84:11b (NLT) says, "The Lord will withhold no good thing from those who do what is right."

Is sex good? It sure is! Is it good for married people? Yes! It is a great blessing for married people to enjoy. Is it good *to* single people? It is for a moment. But is it good *for* single people? Absolutely not! All sexual activity is reserved for celebration within the marriage covenant because that is the plan God had in mind.

You can do it. You can win this war against your mind, body, and spirit.

2 Corinthians 10:4-5 (NIV) shows us how to go to war. "The weapons we fight with are not the weapons of the world. On the contrary, they have divine power to demolish strongholds. We demolish arguments and every pretension that sets itself up against the knowledge of God, and we take captive of every thought to make it obedient to Christ."

***

Write down your takeaway and how you plan to take action:

....

....

....

....

....

PART TWO

ADDITIONAL CHAPTERS

As I (Vernicia) was pulling the rest of this book together, I began having conversations with women who, although they were not having sex with a man, were struggling with masturbation and pornography and wanted accountability partners. This discovery led to the inclusion of these additional chapters to cover more topics regarding the battle for sexual purity that many are facing.

I asked C. Ella Pierce to write these two chapters, and she was gracious enough to do so while sharing her own story of deliverance. A few other women shared their experiences with sexual struggles, and I applaud them for their courage and vulnerability in sharing their truth with all of you.

MASTURBATION

"As for you, you were dead in your trespasses and sins, in which you used to walk when you conformed to the ways of this world and of the ruler of the power of the air, the spirit who is now at work in the sons of disobedience. At one time, we all lived among them, fulfilling the cravings of our flesh and indulging its desires and thoughts. Like the rest, we were by nature children of wrath. But because of His great love for us, God, who is rich in mercy, ⁵made us alive with Christ, even when we were dead in our trespasses. It is by grace you have been saved! And God raised us up with Christ and seated us with Him in the heavenly realms in Christ Jesus..." (Ephesians 2:3-6, NIV).

If you are struggling with masturbation, don't put this book down. Keep reading. I promise I will not condemn you. However, I have a few questions for you to ponder. Is God enough for you? Does He please you more than when you masturbate?

I encourage you to be honest about this. If you answered "no" to these questions, you are in a good place for God to continue to work in you to bring about what pleases Him. For those who admit that pleasing yourself is more important, I applaud you. This isn't easy to admit. It was a bittersweet moment when I admitted this, but God loved me enough to want me to accept my truth. Although I sang the songs of wanting to please Him, secretly, I was still catering to my own needs. In this area of my life, I had not allowed Him to heal me.

Dear one, God already knows your truth, and He's not angry or surprised. He has not and will not ever fall off the throne. He's waiting patiently for you to get real with yourself because unless you do, you cannot get real with Him. He cannot help you in the way He wants to until you bring your truth to Him.

When God delivered me from masturbation, I had been saved for about five years. For all of those five years and at least twenty before that, I was a faithful masturbator. I grew up with both of my parents and my two younger sisters. My childhood wasn't anything out of the ordinary, yet most of my earliest memories were sexual in nature, and I became very sexually curious at an early age.

By the time I was a teenager, I was using a sock to masturbate. But in my late twenties, I discovered water from a tub's running faucet was even more effective and efficient. Masturbation was a welcomed part of my life. It was soothing and pleasing at the moment, but I always felt ashamed afterward. However, that feeling didn't stop me. It filled a void and pleased me in ways that, at that time, nothing else did.

After I became a Christian, I continued with this sexual activity and felt the same way. But this time, I justified it. At the time I came to salvation in Christ, I was no longer in a committed relationship, and when those feelings of guilt, shame, and dirtiness started rising after masturbating, I would say, "I'm not hurting anyone, and I'm not bothering anybody. I'm not fornicating." This went on for years until God began to deal with me.

As I was growing in understanding of Him and His ways, I felt more and more guilt and dirtiness after masturbating, and it wouldn't stop there. I felt convicted after reading a scripture related to holiness or hearing a reference about placing idols before God. Once God told me that pleasing myself had become more important to me than seeking to please Him, I began to get self-righteous with Him. I would say things like, "God, I have given up so much. I am not having sex. I am not having inappropriate relationships with men. Why do I have to give up the one thing that brings me physical pleasure? You made me this way, remember?" God, in all of His mercy and graciousness, allowed me my temper tantrums but remained steadfast in His will, and I struggled more and more with it in a way that I hadn't before.

I found myself wanting to masturbate all the time. It was becoming addictive. I felt like I was in a battle for my life, and I was losing. I knew God wanted me to stop, but I didn't have the power or the resolve to stop. But, God. Philippians 2:13 (NLT) tells us that it is "God is working in you, giving you the desire and the power to do what pleases him." Thank God for God! He is working in us to help us do the thing that is pleasing to Him. Yes, dear one, remember that although He longs to be gracious to you, there is still something you must do in this process. You have to give yourself over to Him, and when you get tired enough, you will know exactly how to do this. He knows exactly how to get us to the end of ourselves.

Dear one, do not despise the presence of a struggle in this journey. Are you struggling with masturbation, or are you satisfied with it? This is a question only you can answer. If a struggle is present, I encourage you to pay attention and realize that you aren't in a place of peace.

Sometimes our greatest victories come from our greatest struggles. Again, do not despise the struggle. Its very presence means something powerful. God may be dealing with you, but you have not yet allowed yourself to come face to face with your truth. I encourage you to present yourself to God as a living sacrifice and be open to what it is that He wants to show you in the midst of your struggle. Just be open. You don't have to agree or disagree at this point. Just remain open to what God wants to do.

I wish I could tell you that one day I got strong enough to resist the temptation to masturbate on my own. Well, just as I didn't save myself, I didn't deliver myself from masturbation either.

A pastor from Uganda came to my church in 2009. Several minutes into his testimony, he went in an unexpected direction and began to share how God had delivered him from masturbation. While he was jumping up, down, and around, proclaiming God's miracle in his life, you could have heard a pin drop in the sanctuary.

Talking about sex, let alone masturbation, from the pulpit was not heard of. I don't even know what the other parishioners looked like, but I know my jaw was on the floor. I found myself totally and simultaneously taken in, taken aback, and immersed within, and unable to draw myself away from the power of his testimony. God allowed this pastor's words to penetrate my heart and fill it with God Himself. God used this pastor's testimony to set me free, and I haven't masturbated since.

Please do not underestimate the power of your testimony. God tells us in Revelation 12:11 that we overcome by the blood of the Lamb and the word of our testimony. That pastor's testimony was from a place of redemption, and he spoke from that power. The same power that rose Jesus from the dead resurrected me from the grave of masturbation that I had been in for almost two decades. If God can do it for me, He will do it for you. Do you believe that He can do it?

Dear one, I was in such a place of torment with doubt, face to face with my weakness and inability to help myself. I had no frame of reference to believe that God would even want to deliver me from such a practice. Now, standing on the other side, I see that He longed to deliver me and that He longs to deliver His children because when He does, we are taken to another level of purity where we can see Him as He longs for us to see Him.

Does temptation come? Yes, it does, but God has graced me to resist, just as James 4:7 (NIV) tells us - "Submit yourselves, then, to God. Resist the devil, and He will flee from you." It is set squarely within my spirit that there is no momentary good feeling worth going back into the place of bondage from which God has delivered me. Nope. Nada. Zilch. I value my freedom too much, and I don't want to go back into slavery to my flesh. At the time of this writing, that moment of deliverance was ten years ago. God has been faithful.

Even though God has kept me, dear ones, I am still on my walk to purity. God is dealing with me in my thought life. But, I know that if He did it before, He can do it again. I have to stop and remind myself of my testimony because, again, we overcome by the blood of the Lamb and the word of our testimony. Here are some tips I used to remind myself when I am waiting on freedom:

Is this [thought/act] a sin?

The Bible doesn't specifically mention masturbation, although it does mention sexual immorality. What matters most is that you need to know what the Holy Spirit is saying to you. Is the Holy Spirit bringing conviction? Remember, James 4:17 (NIV) tells us that if "If anyone, then, knows the good they ought to do and doesn't do it, it is sin for them." Romans 14:23 (NKJV) tells us that "whatever is not from faith is sin."

Am I still in agreement with this [thought/act]?

If so, I need to pray and ask God to help me come out of agreement with it.

Sample prayer:

Father,

I come before You believing that You are God of all. You are my God, and I am Yours. I thank You for Your Son Jesus and His shed blood over my life, and I thank You for the gift of the Holy Spirit living within me. God, forgive me for my sin against You and help me to come out of agreement with this sin so that I can repent with sincerity and honesty. Help me to hate this sin as You hate sin. Help me to love holiness as You love holiness. I thank You for helping me and loving me more and more into Your truth.

Amen.

Am I struggling with this [thought/act]?

If there is no struggle, ask yourself if you're at peace with it. If you feel you are at peace with it, then keep seeking God about it. He knows the plans He has to prosper you and not harm you. He can help you overcome this struggle and restore your life to its original design as you surrender to Him.

If you are not at peace, and you find yourself feeling convicted, talk to God about this struggle. Ask Him to deliver you and believe that He will. He will bring His Word to you. He will bring His people to you. He will help you because He loves you and longs to be gracious to you.

Reach out to people you can trust. Seek advice through pastoral counsel, an accountability partner, and/or a prayer partner. It is very important to not go through this alone. When I was delivered, I spoke to no one. In 2009, talking about masturbation was unheard of amongst my Christian friends and family. Today, there is more freedom and openness regarding sexual matters, even within the church. Take advantage of this and make sure you seek out the support you need as the Lord leads you.

Remember, there is no condemnation for those who are in Christ Jesus (Romans 8:1, ESV). Wait on God. Blessed are those who wait for Him (Isaiah 30:18, NIV). Psalm 103:14

(NIV) tells us that God "knows how we are formed, He remembers that we are dust." These words are not a pass for us to sin, but they encourage us to take our struggles to Him and to wait on Him in faith because He remains faithful (2 Timothy 2:13, NIV) even when we are not.

At the time of this writing, our world is experiencing a shift in the perception of masturbation. Reports are touting the health benefits and normalcy of masturbation[3]. As Christian singles, we are to give ourselves over to self-control, a fruit of the Spirit. If we lack self-control, then we are to seek God, acknowledge this weakness, and believe by faith that He will honor our request.

Remember, He longs to be gracious to us. Finally, please always be mindful of the need for purity in our lives and continue to seek God and His Word for what this looks like for you. Matthew 5:8 (NIV) tells us that "Blessed are the pure in heart, for they shall see God."

Jillian's Story

I discovered pornography around eleven years old. The discovery was completely innocent, and initially, I didn't involve any sexual thoughts. But I wish someone would have talked to me about the fact that this sexual feeling I had existed. I wish someone would have told me how God created sex to bond a married couple together. I don't remember the timing, but at some point, I was sexually molested. That is when I became more curious, and my thoughts started becoming more sexually focused.

I have learned that, along with other hormones, sex releases a bonding hormone called oxytocin. These hormones not only make us feel good but also create a bond between us and the person we are with. The best way I can think of to describe sex is that it is like a "glue" to help hold a married couple together. This is why having sex early in a relationship and before marriage is such a dangerous thing. We are bonding ourselves to an infatuation or to the person we think we are with but don't really know yet. In the same way, when a person masturbates to a fantasy, they are binding themselves to that fantasy. We create a "glue" to a person or relationship that does not exist. Anytime we live in a fantasy in any part of our life, it can be detrimental to our reality.

When talking about masturbation, we've often mistakenly asked, "Is it wrong?" Instead, we should be asking ourselves, "What fantasy are we bonding to and why?" Ask God to help you understand yourself. Ask him to show you your heart. Remember that God is gentle and kind to you, so as you evaluate your motivations, be gentle and kind to yourself. Also, be honest with yourself.

Here are some questions that can help you process:

1. Why do I feel the need to masturbate?

2. Am I trying to escape my reality?

3. What feels better about this fantasy than my reality?

4. Do I want to create a deeper bond with something that does not exist?

5. Do I truly believe God understands what I'm going through?

Remember, your physical longing for sex is a desire created by God, and it is PURE and GOOD. When it comes to lust, we need to run (1 Corinthians 6:18, NLT). We also need to run from thoughts of coveting our neighbor's wife or husband. But let's stop trying to stifle or run from our God-given longings. Instead, let's use them as another opportunity that God has given us to shine a light into our hearts, exposing the lies we believe and replacing them with the truth of His Word.

The fact that I feel alone in having strong sexual feelings is a struggle for me. The fact that I think that "normal" girls don't feel this way and wonder if something is wrong with me makes me sad. The Christian culture is so open about godly men having a strong sex drive, but silent on godly women who do, and I feel like I can never be honest or tell anyone how I feel. Sometimes, I feel like I don't belong in my body.

To you who are struggling with masturbation:

I just want you to know that you are normal. These desires are normal. Sexual feelings are a beautiful thing that God created. Invite God into your journey and allow Him to show you why He created this beautiful, pure, and mysterious part of you. Your desires do not have to take you down a path of confusion and darkness. Instead of getting frustrated with yourself or with your desires, let them lead you to a God who is loving, strong, and ready to share the secrets of the kingdom with you. Know that "the LORD confides in those who fear him; He makes his covenant known to them" (Psalm 25:14, NIV).

References

1. www.businesswire.com/news/home/20190424005815/en/Global-Sex-Toys-Market-2019-2023-Growing-Awareness; accessed August 3, 2019

2. https://www.healthline.com/health/masturbation-side-effects#benefits; accessed August 7, 2019

3. https://www.healthychildren.org/English/ages-stages/gradeschool/puberty/Pages/Masturbation.aspx;accessed August 5, 2019

4. https://www.cru.org/us/en/train-and-grow/life-and-relationships/men/flesh/whats-up-with-masturbation.html; accessed August 7, 2019

5. https://www.focusonthefamily.com/family-qa/questions-and-concerns-about-masturbation/; accessed August 7, 2019

***

Write down your takeaway and how you plan to take action:

....

....

....

....

PORNOGRAPHY

I could ask the darkness to hide me and the light around me to become night — but even in darkness, I cannot hide from you..." (Psalm 139:11

The negative effects of pornography are elusive and delayed. Initially, your mind is engaged, and your body is aroused and, usually, through some form of masturbation, your flesh's lustful demands are satisfied, and the thrill subsides. As my father used to say to my younger sisters and me when we were teenagers, "the devil never comes to you ugly." He was right.

The devil comes to entice, appeal to, and entrap you by looking, smelling, sounding, tasting, and feeling good to your flesh. While He seduces you, He lures you in and secures you tightly into loyal bondage to him. Matthew 6:24 (NIV) says, "No one can serve two masters. Either you will hate the one and love the other, or you will be devoted to the one and despise the other." Where does loyal bondage to the enemy take us?

R. Nicholas Black shares the following from *What's Wrong With a Little Porn When You're Single*:

"With or without marriage, pornography can lead to sexual addiction. It is the visual equivalent of crystal meth - a powerful but destructive high that creates the craving for an even bigger high. Like drug use that starts out casually but escalates over time, it becomes a desperate, compelling force that overrides all sanity. As with all addictions, no one starts out thinking He will become addicted to porn, but that is where it ends up for all too many men and women..."

Grace's Story

It all started when I was nine years old at a sleepover with a group of fellow Girl Scouts. One of the girls put in a pornographic video after the adults were asleep. I do not remember the details at all, but I do remember something was awakened in me after that point. Afterward, I would find magazines hidden by my grandfather and stepfather.

At thirteen, I started experimenting with boys, but I did not start looking at pornography until I was probably sixteen years old. Eventually, I began looking at images and watching short videos on the internet when I was alone in my room. However, I do remember that it was exhilarating initially. After that pursuit, I kept looking for that first feeling of ecstasy to no avail. I did think it was wrong but not enough to stop.

Porn provided a sexual experience when I was not having an actual sexual experience with a man. It closed me off from pursuing intimate human relationships. Rather than to risk establishing relationships with complicated human beings (both male and female), I retreated to what I thought I could control. I thought I pursued pornography on my terms.

Pornography fulfilled temporary physical and emotional desires, which I found helpful. However, the harm was more permanent. Pornography left me incapable of developing genuine human relationships. I have minimized God's Word and desire for my life and the lives of others. I have deliberately disobeyed Him and encouraged disobedience, deception, and harm to others by seeking counterfeit intimacy.

Truth began to settle in my heart when I started studying the Bible, listening to Christian radio programs that talked about the direct impacts of porn, and ultimately the Holy Spirit. Pornography was never discussed in church, but God never abandoned me. I always felt guilty for what I was doing. However, when I started to feel numb before and after viewing pornography, God strategically put me in places of ultimate dependence on Him.

Through sequential experiences of physical loss of property, health issues, the threat of my safety, and the loss of a loved one over a six-month period, I sought God like I never had before. Because I did not feel safe in my home, I would leave the radio on the Bible Broadcast Network, day and night. There were hymns, bible teaching, and prayers filling the house. I prayed morning and night. I wrote in a journal—which I had never done. I was starting to open myself to God's voice.

Then one day, I was listening to the radio broadcast program, Family Life Today, and the host asked the guest, "What is the most courageous thing you have ever done?" The guest answered that it was sharing his struggle with pornography with his wife and accountability group. I was frozen stiff as I listened to that conversation. I had heard this discussion so many times before and brushed it off. I had said to myself, "I can overcome this on my own. I can't tell anyone, or my life will be over," but this time was different. Never before had I felt such conviction. I could not move unless I confessed my sin to God and asked his forgiveness, and I had to confess my sin to fellow believers—including leadership. It was so hard, but freeing. I could not fix this on my own.

Almost forty years have passed since I saw that first movie. Nothing was fixed. Keeping my addiction secret just gave it power. I allowed my shame to come before God's ultimate will for my life. I lived a life of mediocrity because of fear. I am still in recovery. However, just having the opportunity to share my story publicly is showing God's love and concern for me and all of you too.

My recommendation to you is after you've confessed your sins to God and repented, seek an accountability partner. We are not meant to walk this path to freedom alone. Through prayer, ask God to give you wisdom and point you to someone who can come alongside you in this journey. Someone who will speak life, who will pray for you and with you, who will ask you the hard questions.

Seek counseling. Transforming our minds is challenging when we do not know any other way to think. A professional can help walk alongside you in the process. Finally, remove what may tempt you. This may mean anything where you have internet access: your computer, cable TV/Streaming sticks, and cell phone. Any type of idle unproductive time is not good.

Most importantly, I find that I have to prioritize seeking God through prayer and the study of His Word. When I skip that, I start allowing idols in my life and well...God does not share His glory. I want to honor God in my life, whatever that takes. I believe that He is good, and He wants the best. It may not look the way I want to look or happen how I want it to happen, but God is good and faithful. I have to trust him. Where else am I going to go? There is no other place. You (Lord) have the words of eternal life (John 6:68, NIV).

Looking Again

"Catch for us the foxes, the little foxes that ruin the
vineyards, our vineyards that are in bloom"
(Song of Songs 2:15, NIV)

For years, this verse's meaning has eluded me. On the surface, I understood "little foxes" to mean distractions, and, essentially, this is what it means. See below a Matthew Henry commentary explaining this scripture:

The first risings of sinful thoughts and desires, the beginnings of trifling pursuits which waste time, trifling visits, small departures from truth, whatever would admit some conformity to the world; all these, and many more, are little foxes which must be removed. This is a charge to believers to mortify their sinful appetites and passions, which are as little foxes that destroy their graces and comforts and crush good beginnings. Whatever we find a hindrance to us in that which is good, we must put away.

Thank you, Mr. Matthew Henry. How doth we put these little foxes out of our vineyard?

First, we must understand that "therefore, there is now no condemnation to those who are in Christ Jesus" (Romans 8:1, NIV). And God remembers that we are dust (Psalms 103:14, NIV). Second, we must understand that the vineyard is the place of blessing within which God alone has brought us into for intimacy with Him. Third, we must be willing to admit that there are little foxes lurking in our vineyard, and we must look to our protector and deliverer to help us rid the vineyard of the unwelcome intruder. But wait. Is the intruder truly unwelcomed? Are we allowing things of this world to enter and influence us?

When we are too close, we cannot see the full picture. When we agree with the intruder, there's no struggle, and, from our perspective, there's nothing to repent of.

[Stats]

Nearly two-thirds of Christian men and a third of Christian women admit to struggling with pornography on a regular basis. It's wreaking havoc in the lives of many believers. https://www.messengercourses.com/porn-free#offer

Maylissa's Story

Pornography is harmful because it distorts a person's view of what intimacy really is. What many people don't know is that there is so much violence in pornography. Several of the actors are starting to come forward with the truth that they aren't even able to perform the various sexual positions and scenes that the producers want without first using drugs and alcohol. There is nothing glamorous about it, and, sadly, so many people look to it as an example of what they want their sex lives to be like.

I experienced sexual abuse during most of my childhood as I was in and out of foster care and group homes. I began masturbating when I was around seven or eight years old as a means to escape the surrounding trauma. It was a natural thing that I did as a coping mechanism, and afterward, I would go to sleep. I always seemed to have one foot in the sexual entertainment industry, because my mother was a dancer, and I was exposed to people and situations that I should never have been exposed to as a child.

At the age of fifteen, I was a part of the sex industry and didn't even realize I was being abused. In time, I began to control how I was being used as well as the money that I made, and because of that, I was blind to what was happening. All of that was creating a barrier that would make it extremely difficult to ever have a healthy sex life.

With the lifestyle that I lived, pornography was a normal afterthought that was ever-present in my world. I thought pornography displayed what sex was supposed to be like and what men and women desired in sex. I didn't realize pornography was teaching me to be an object for men.

Years later, I got married, and my husband often watched porn. I didn't care to engage in watching it with him, but it didn't bother me that He watched it. Porn is highly addictive, and you don't know when you start becoming addicted. It can sneak up on you, distorting your brain, and translating intimacy into something that is unhealthy. Porn makes you think that what you see on screen is real when it's actually a wicked fantasy.

With all that I went through, God's love never failed. My husband and I weren't religious at the time, but as parents, we wanted to see good examples of healthy families and figured what better place to see good families than the church. The way God pursued us was amazing.

Someone at my job invited me to the same church that someone had invited my husband to. We accepted the invitation and began going to that church. After attending church for a few weeks, God gripped my heart. I surrendered to Him and trusted Him as my Lord and Savior. My husband made the same choice, and it changed our lives.

Turning to Christ didn't change our sex life overnight, but eventually, my husband began to crave a healthy sex life with me. I believe his desire came from his relationship with God. When you're close to God, He begins to show you things about yourself, as well as things that you need to improve in your life.

I had grown to the point that I hated sex. It was disgusting to me, and I even went as far as to tell my husband that He had my permission to have sex outside of our marriage as long as He came home to me. I thank God that my husband had a connection with Him and that He didn't take me up on my offer. Instead, He began to pray for me and our sex life. God made it very clear and spoke to him in his spirit, "If you want a healthy sex life, then you need to give this pornography to me." My husband broke down, turned to God, and from that day, He never watched another film.

I am thankful because I wasn't at a place in my life where I was ready to address these issues. I had accepted our dysfunctional sex life as normal. God soon began transforming my life even more. He helped me forgive the abusers of my past and release all of my past hurts to Him. My husband and I have been married for seventeen years, and I praise God for the transformation that has occurred in our intimacy and our marriage. He makes all things new!

If you watch pornography, I urge you to seek God and ask Him to help you overcome this very dangerous addiction. What many people don't understand is that pornography hijacks your brain. Pornography works like a drug. Our brain produces a chemical called dopamine. Dopamine is like a shot that the brain gets as the person becomes desensitized. The images that satisfied last month are not going to have the same effect the next month. As time goes on, the person will be prone to look for more hard-core pornography. It's like a rabbit hole you can't get out of easily. The person continues to desire that surge of dopamine over and over. They will begin to spiral downward as time goes on, pleasing their brain and looking for more gratifying images to reward themselves while descending into a deteriorating addiction.

When it comes to being free from this addiction, one of the important things to realize is that God didn't design pornography at all. It is not normal behavior, and it is not how He created us to live in a loving, intimate relationship. Please know that if you are watching pornography and you're unable to stop, you are undoubtedly addicted. Just as a person who is addicted to drugs needs help to overcome their addiction, it would behoove you to seek help for your pornography addiction as well. It is important to reach out to someone you trust, go to therapy, pray about it, and fight this full-on to bring it into the light. When we keep things in the dark, we can't find healing there. We have to shed light on it and bring it out in the open. When we keep it covered up, satan is free to wreak havoc in our lives while we suffer and fall in silence.

Statistics show there is a 30% rise in women addicted to pornography, and the numbers continue to rise in both males and females. To combat this, being active in your church is always awesome, and it's good to have other activities going on in your life, such as volunteering or helping other people. If that's not of interest to you, get into sports, or find other hobbies to participate in. If you are having a hard time online, it may sound strange, but get rid of the internet. Protect yourself and eliminate any access to it.

You may ask, what does the Bible have to say about all of this? The Bible does address sexual sin. Bottom line, pornography ultimately hurts the person who is watching it and those they are in an intimate relationship with. Romans 1:24-27 (NIV) says, "Therefore God gave them over in the sinful desires of their heart to sexual purity for the degrading of their bodies of one another. They exchanged the truth about God for a lie and worshiped and served created things rather than the Creator, who is forever praised. Because of this, God gave them over to shameful lust. Even their women exchanged natural sexual relations for unnatural ones. In the same way, the men also abandoned natural relations with women who were inflamed with lust for one another. Men committed shameful acts with other men and received in themselves the due penalty for their error."

The last part of this verse hit home for me because of the realization that pornography hurts not only your partner, but also your body, your mind, your soul, and your spirit. It is important to understand that you are harming yourself when you're watching pornography. You are harming your future relationships, your future husband or wife, and your children or future children.

I've heard cases where men were so addicted to pornography, and because the regular pornography they were watching wasn't satisfying them anymore, they actually started to see their daughter as a sexual object and abused them. This is a part of that downward spiral. Years before pornography was in their lives, these men probably would've never thought of abusing their own child, but this is what happens when pornography hijacks your brain. You're bringing your brain to places where it was never intended to go.

Today, God has redeemed my life. I help women leave the sex industry, and I fight against human trafficking. It's amazing that I'm helping other women get out of the thing that tried to destroy me. And I'm loving on them where they're at and encouraging them to do something better with their lives.

With all of this, there is hope. Sexual intimacy was made to be shared between two people who love each other and enter into a marital covenant. It is clear that God doesn't approve of pornography. He loves you so much, and He's preparing someone for you. Whether you're in a relationship or not, you have to trust God with your sexuality and believe that He has someone that He is preparing for you for the rest of your life when you get married. That special person is worth waiting for to have that marital bliss you will experience when you wait on God.

***

Write down your takeaway and how you plan to take action:

....

....

....

....

....

More Courageous Faith Stories

These are the stories of some of the bravest women I (Vernicia) know who have had similar thoughts, feelings, and behaviors as you have experienced. You are not alone, and you certainly are not the only one.

Stacey's Story

As a young teen, I didn't value myself. I had very little self-esteem and didn't realize the value of what I was giving away or opening myself up to. I was a believer and was told not to have sex, but I didn't understand why. I wish I had known how valuable I was.

I met my first real boyfriend in my sophomore year in high school, and that is when my sexual experience began. We were together for a couple of years. Over time, our physical relationship progressed, and we had sex.

After our relationship ended, I had another boyfriend who I had a sexual relationship with, and I also had a couple of nights of too much drinking where I ended up with people I hardly knew. The use of alcohol caused me to be more relaxed in environments where opportunities were more prevalent. It grieves my heart deeply when I look back on that version of myself and how I gave myself away so easily.

I know I am forgiven because I no longer feel ashamed or condemned. Thankfully, I have seen the redemption of the Lord in this area of my life. He makes all things new!

My husband and I fought hard to stay pure when we were dating. We were physical but never crossed the line. It wasn't easy, but we valued each other and didn't want our future marriage to be tainted in any way. Joining with someone in sex has huge emotional, physical, and spiritual implications, which is a blessing within marriage but deadly outside of marriage. Sex is such a powerful force in marriage because that is God's design. When we come together, it is a powerful act of warfare - walls get broken down, communication improves, and marriage is strengthened. No wonder the enemy has sought to pervert sex and glamorize it outside of marriage.

To my younger self, I would say you are so valuable. You have so much to offer beyond your physical appearance and your body. Your sexuality and body are a gift. Honor yourself, honor the Lord, and honor your future husband. Marriage is awesome, and sex inside of marriage is awesome! Do not uncover yourself. The marriage covenant, commitment, and covering is the way the Father designed for you to experience that level of intimacy and vulnerability. Trust Him, trust what He says about sex. He designed it; He knows how it works best. Read Song of Solomon. Father God is not holding out on you. He is rewarding you.

Victoria's Story

My sexual experience began in childhood with inappropriate touching, and from that point on, I was very curious. Unfortunately, I continued to have sexual experiences as a preteen and participated in intercourse for the first time when I was fifteen years old.

I didn't know my worth or think about my future apart from the men in my life. I thought my life would really begin when I got married. I didn't realize that premarital sex had a negative impact on me emotionally, spiritually, and mentally.

I believed sex would save or further a relationship, but my hopes were dashed many times. I didn't realize how sexual acts bonded me to men I did not have a future with. Learning that I could start over, be free from sexual sin, and be made whole gave me hope and a new lease on life.

Practicing abstinence is not as much about what I'm not doing (abstaining from sex) but what I *am* doing, e.g., walking in wholeness, protecting my mind/body/heart/future. It wasn't until I began practicing abstinence that I was able to identify an unhealthy relationship versus a healthy relationship.

I realized that my sex drive was from God, and that temptation helped me to recognize my need for intimacy. It also caused me to long for a day when I would not be tempted any longer. Once I realized my worth and stopped settling for less than I deserved, I was able to trust the Lord and hold my head up. I was confident in my decision to abstain and able to maintain my boundaries. I realized the Lord wanted to use me to offer support and encouragement to others. God showed me He had a plan all along. I returned to school and finished my undergraduate and graduate degree.

If I could tell my younger self anything, I would tell her about the value of saving sex for marriage. I would tell her to value her worth and not settle for less than she deserves. If I were advising my younger self, I would surround myself with like-minded people who could become part of my inner circle and provide friendship and accountability.

Chandra's Story

My sexual experience began with being fondled as a teenage girl. I had vowed not to have sex until marriage but didn't know sperm swam. My son's father and I messed around often, and I got pregnant without being penetrated. I was shocked and angry with my mother for not teaching me about my body and sex. I was three months pregnant when the doctor told me I was pregnant.

I believed that fondling was okay as long as I wasn't having sexual intercourse. I didn't know the importance of valuing my body and not allowing a man to touch my private parts. I believed the lie that God wouldn't forgive me for making a mistake, so I got married because I was pregnant. I believed the lie that God didn't love me, and I would go to hell if I had a child out of wedlock.

I was set free by the truth that Jesus loves me. He forgives me and died to set me free. Sanctification is a process. I will sin, but if I confess my sins, He is faithful and just to forgive me (1 John 1:7-9, NKJV). Also, if I confess my sins to others, I will be healed (James 5:16a, NIV).

The truth of God's grace has revolutionized my life. I no longer live by the law but by God's grace. I help others balance truth and grace so they can live free. I've had the privilege of speaking life to my son when He and his now-wife faced an unplanned pregnancy. Today, I help women who struggle with sexual sin.

I would tell the younger me to trust God, believe that His love is greater than anyone's love, and surround herself with godly people who have her best interest in mind. I would tell her to find a community that is authentic, vulnerable, human, honest, merciful, and non-judgmental. To my younger self, I would say, "value who you are - uniquely and beautifully created as a daughter of Christ."

Yolanda's Story

My sexual experience began like many others. I was dating a young man whom I believed loved me and only wanted to be with me, possibly forever. I was also curious and wanted to be recognized as the "cool" girl, not the religious "good girl."

The lies I believed weren't actually verbally spoken directly to me. They were based on society's view of sex:

- Everyone is having sex.

- If you don't have sex with your significant other, he'll cheat on you or cut off the relationship.

In my twenties, I was set free by these truths:

- God forgives.

- It is possible to be in a relationship with someone equally yoked and willing to abstain from sex until marriage.

- Having a strong relationship with God provides you with companionship, love, and acceptance that was once sought after through sex.

Abstaining from sex with my husband while we were dating has given us a foundation that is based on growing together spiritually, the ability to genuinely love one another unconditionally, and a strong friendship.

If I had to tell my younger self about sex, I would tell her that having sex before marriage should not take place regardless of friends, significant others, or even what society may say. The spiritual and emotional baggage that comes along with premarital sex can create obstacles and challenges (like trust and commitment issues) throughout one's marriage.

Ann's Story

There have always been undertones and undercurrents of sexualization in my life, and I can't tell you why. Before I actually had sex with a man at the age of nineteen, I had been sexual in many other ways.

As a child, I remember walking in on my parents while they slept naked, or at least they appeared to be sleep, on top of the covers of their bed. Their bedroom door was wide open. I remember walking in the room to sneak a peek at them.

Also, I remember seeing pornography and being intrigued by it. I don't remember watching it after that one time, but visually, I'd imagine people having sex. My sister and I played husband and wife, and I allowed my nephew to molest me when He was around six or seven while I pretended to be asleep. And as a teenager, I would masturbate off and on for years.

At sixteen, I had my first boyfriend. We never had intercourse, but we messed around and were sexually involved in other activities that would prevent me from getting pregnant. Years later, I did get pregnant and had two children by a man. After that, my kids went to live with their dad, and He was able to get full custody because He manipulated the circumstances, and I allowed it. I was afraid of him, but he would still have sex with me if He wanted.

I accepted Christ on October 11, 2003 and had sex with my children's father in December. The following month, January 2004, I had sex with two men, one on the 17th and the other on the 31st. I was impregnated during one of those encounters, and my baby was due in October. Right before I gave birth to my youngest child, I had sex again several times with my older children's father. Four months after my youngest daughter was born, a paternity test was conducted, and she met her father for the first time.

Since 2004, I have not had sex. Since 2008, I have not masturbated. Now, God is dealing with my thoughts and desires, getting to the root of the sexual behavior I experienced even before having sex.

I believed that sex was love and good sex meant that it was really, really love. My parents didn't talk to me about sex. The only thing my father said was if I got pregnant, I'd have to go out and get a job. My mother was so nervous when she tried to talk to me about sex at sixteen. I told her I hadn't done anything, and she was relieved.

More than that, my dad always told me that Christians were hypocrites. There was nothing and no one to tell me about relationships God's way or how I was supposed to relate to myself and men. I believed in the secular music of the day. If it felt good, it was good. I believed whatever a man told me at face value. I wanted so desperately to be loved.

God and His truth set me free. Nothing else. Before God delivered me from masturbation, I didn't have any concept of being free from anything. How would I have known that freedom was possible? I felt God nudging me to stop masturbating and to stop making myself and my need for pleasure and fulfillment an idol before Him. But I had no idea that He could and would take away the desire to masturbate. It was after hearing someone share about their deliverance from masturbation that I was freed from it. Oh, I have been tempted; but, when I think about what God has delivered me from and the bondage I was in, I just shake my head and remind myself that it is not worth getting back into bondage. It's just not that bad yet, and by God's grace, it won't be that bad ever again.

When I got pregnant after getting saved, God had a plan to restore me. In fact, He knew that I was going to get pregnant. I didn't know it then, but He used the birth of my daughter to redeem me. He gave me her name. I thought it was for her, but I realized that her name is a reminder to me about how He feels about me and her. Her name comes from 1 Corinthians 6:19-20 (KJV), "What? Know ye not that your body is the temple of the Holy Ghost, which is in you, which ye have of God, and ye are not your own? For ye are bought with a price; therefore glorify God in your body, and in your spirit, which are God's."

The Message version breaks it down nicely: "There's more to sex than mere skin on skin. Sex is as much spiritual mystery as physical fact. As written in Scripture, The two become one." Since we want to become spiritually one with the Master, we must not pursue the kind of sex that avoids commitment and intimacy, leaving us lonelier than ever—the kind of sex that can never "become one."

There is a sense in which sexual sins are different from all others. In sexual sin, we violate the sacredness of our own bodies, these bodies that were made for God-given and God-modeled love for "becoming one" with another. Didn't you realize that your body is a sacred place, the place of the Holy Spirit? Don't you see that you can't live however you please, squandering what God paid such a high price for? The physical part of you is not some piece of property belonging to the spiritual part of you. God owns the whole works, so let people see God in and through your body."

These scriptures have also helped me:

"If we confess our sins, He is faithful and just to forgive us our sins and to cleanse us from all unrighteousness" (1 John 1:9, KJV).

"Confess your faults one to another, and pray one for another, that ye may be healed. The effectual fervent prayer of a righteous man availeth much" (James 5:16, KJV).

"For God is working in you, giving you the desire and the power to do what pleases him" (Philippians 2:13, NLT).

"That is what the Scriptures mean when they say, 'No eye has seen, no ear has heard, and no mind has imagined what God has prepared for those who love him'" (1 Corinthians 2:9, NLT).

There are so many more scriptures I could share, especially those dealing with renewing our minds and taking thoughts captive to the obedience of Christ.

I have felt very insecure about my future because of how sexualized I was in the past. I've often wondered how I will be a good and faithful wife, but only God knows. My current walk is to trust what His Word says about me because nothing in my life and nothing in my past, says that I am going to overcome any of this. But that's what faith is about. That's what hope is. Abraham hoped against hope, and his faith made him our spiritual father. I am walking in Abraham's shoes in the way Christ made for us both.

I wish I had told myself to wait, to take all the despairing energy that caused me to seek out what I thought was love and seek after God just as hard. The momentary thrill is just not worth living without peace. My walk with God is the only component of my life that brings me overwhelming joy. Nothing else can compare. But, if you have never tasted God's love for yourself, of course, you'll be thirsty. Of course, you'll be hungry, seeking to fill that yearning and squelch that need for attention and affection. I would also tell myself to look beyond what I feel and what I see because there is so much more.

Dana Che's Story

The summer before my senior year in high school, I lost my "V" card. That's virginity card, for those who don't know. As an avid supporter of the "wait until marriage" crew, I never imagined I'd actually have sex outside of marriage. However, my boyfriend and I had been dating several years, and as our relationship intensified, so did its physical nature.

I think I believed the lie that sex would bring us closer together. While it is true that sex creates a powerful soul tie, I found that sex actually brought along some unforeseen issues (emotional roller coasters and a loss of respect for one another), which in turn caused us to begin to grow farther apart.

I actually married my boyfriend, and after a few years of marital dysfunction, I realized that my disobedience to God's Word brought about some problems we were facing (our communication, lack of respect for one another, and lack of true intimacy). It wasn't until I repented of those decisions and we re-purified our marriage that things began to change. What set me free was the realization that God loved me, and this truth became heart knowledge, not just head knowledge.

I have compassion for couples trying to stay abstinent. It's hard. I have dedicated a large portion of my ministry to healthy relationships, including discussing sexual issues in dating and marital relationships. I share honestly and openly with couples, encouraging them to conduct their relationships God's way to avoid those unforeseen hurdles that disobedience brings about.

I would advise the younger me to "not awaken love until the time is right" (Song of Solomon 8:4, NLT). I would tell my younger self not to get heavily involved in a romantic relationship so young. Discover who you are first. Be sure your identity is set before you try to fully love someone else. And finally, do things God's way. It's always the best way.

Samantha's Story

I think to accurately explain how my experience with sex began, some background to my life is necessary. I grew up in a strict Christian home, and my parents were pastors. They instilled a healthy fear that abstaining from sex was the only way to maintain my purity. There was never any real explanation for that, other than sex was something my parents forbade because it was against God's Word.

The older I got, the more fearful I became. I was terrified that the Bible said we are not to have sex before marriage. I was taught that this sin was a "big" sin, and I would go to hell if I had sex before marriage. There was no redemption. That in itself was hard to deal with, so I chose to remain abstinent.

When I was about fifteen years old, I decided to look into the Bible myself to see what the scripture really says about premarital sex. I had just started high school, and there was a super cute football player who wanted to be my boyfriend. He was older, so I thought it was important for me to know about sex if it ever came up.

What I found was not condemning at all. It actually was specific to the beauty of marriage and oneness in a way that I had never heard. In all the places where sexual immorality was involved, the people suffered in ways they didn't necessarily have to. I felt empowered that it was not just about abstaining from sex; it was about keeping something that was designed for my pleasure with my husband.

The first time I was ever tempted to do anything was with that striking football player, hanging out at his house watching movies. His parents were home but outside in the garden. He kissed me and put his hands around my waist. I got butterflies in my stomach. The next thing I knew, He was trying to take my shirt off. I freaked out! I had never been that exposed in front of a boy before, and I was embarrassed — even if I had wanted to do anything. I asked him to slow down, and respectfully He did.

That was the first and last time I let myself feel like I was not in control of that kind of situation. I never let myself get to that point again until I was eighteen years old. I had been dating this guy who was again older than me. We had been together for two years, and I was now a senior.

I had such a hard, violent relationship with my mother that I fully invested any bit of happy emotion into the relationship with this guy. At the onset of dating, we agreed that He would respect my decision to wait until I was married. At our second anniversary mark, He proposed, and I was elated. I couldn't imagine my life without him. We were growing up and learning about the hardships of life together. He was helping support me through the abuse I was facing at home. I knew He would be the one I would spend my life with.

After we told our families about our desire to get married, they were divided. His family was completely supportive. Mine, not so much. My mother said He was a loser and did not think we should even be together.

I tried my best to move forward with excitement. We began making plans. He moved from his parents' house and got an apartment far away from both of our families. I did research on colleges close to his new place. The first time I visited him was after I had a terrible fight with my mom about him. I was so angry and vulnerable. I went to his house. We talked about our life together, about being free from the turmoil once I graduated, and we got married. That night, I decided that since we were getting married, I could give myself to him. And we had sex for the first time.

A few months went by, and my mom and I had an encounter that was life-changing for both of us. My mom tried to take my life. When I survived, I was forever changed. When I told him what happened, He was changed as well, but not in the way I would have hoped. He decided that He did not want to deal with my drama-filled life anymore and was no longer interested in getting married.

I was devastated. Sex seemed justifiable when I considered the idea that I was going to marry him. He would be my husband soon, but now that we weren't getting married, I couldn't get back what I gave away.

This sent me down a path that made me feel like I did not need to protect myself from having random sex. I had already given it away. The deed was done. There was no redemption. It was not until later when I decided to really dedicate my life to God that I realized I did not need to be bound by that idea.

Shortly after, I finally met the man who was going to commit his life to me - my future husband. We were engaged after a year of dating, and I was growing closer to God during this time. I felt an intense conviction from the Holy Spirit, who was telling me that I could abstain from having sex with him until we were married. I felt certain that He would wait because honoring his commitment to God and himself was his priority. Keeping ourselves abstinent until we got married was the best thing for our relationship. We grew spiritually in ways that I don't think we would have had we allowed ourselves to slip into sexual sin.

Looking back, I would tell my younger self that since I waited that long, I should have held out even longer. It would have been worth it. There is a sweet intimacy that comes with marriage, and my only regret is that I did not wait until I was married. I was not missing out on anything by not participating in sexual activity.

After some time, it became clear to me that I could have waited. Instead, I gave something of myself to another man that I wish I had only given to my husband. I know now that there is redemption. All I had to do was surrender myself to God and ask for forgiveness and self-control.

I asked for God to give me back what I gave away and to give back what I took from him in that process, and He did. I actually felt something physical when confessing those things from my mouth with the truest sincerity. If you have made the same mistake, know that God can and will restore you as you commit to saving this precious gift for the man who will ask for your hand in marriage.

Jessica's Story

My first sexual experience happened during my freshman year in high school after a sophomore boy showed interest in me. He was more experienced in the relationship department than I was, and I believed that He could "show me" how it all worked. I was naïve and needy for attention and affection.

In my broken world, He seemed to be all that I had longed for. My parents had not been affectionate growing up and then divorced quickly when I was in middle school, leaving me very confused and hungry for answers about love. It felt great to be seen as attractive and to be desired by a cute boy on the football team. I believed the lie that this was somehow a rite of passage for high school and a way to be normal among my peers and the unspoken expectation of a boyfriend/girlfriend relationship.

We started hanging out, and the guy showed me what the "bases" were in getting physically close. It all seemed okay, although risqué. It was exciting, too, until He asked if we could have sex. I was uncomfortable and didn't know what to think. It felt like a huge label came with having sex that I didn't like but feeling loved and desired was a bigger force.

Thankfully, the relationship ended with some close calls but not actual intercourse. In my next relationship, as a junior in high school, I dated a boy from another school, and He became my everything. I bought into the lie that having sex with him would somehow show our commitment to the relationship and be proof of our love and value to one another. I remember learning about sexual experiences in health class and having shameful thoughts about what I had done with this boy. It felt like I compromised who I was, but I didn't know how to make it stop.

I had grown up in the church and had professed Christ as my Savior in middle school. I had taken bold steps and gone on mission trips and attended youth group. I received compliments on my character, leadership abilities, and my bright future ahead, serving God. I didn't know much about sex and dating other than what I had observed and pretended I knew.

The biblical truth that sex was forbidden outside of marriage became a suggestion for me rather than a loving protection over me and my future. I don't know how I didn't get pregnant or get an STD, but I began to see the effects of my decision to compromise my body with sex as my desire for church and youth group became sporadic. I focused more on trying to earn value and worth through my successes at sports and climbing the social ladder among my peers. I developed an instinctive desire to hide my true inner self and prove that I was a "good girl" to others around me. Being a chameleon became exhausting.

Thankfully, after that boyfriend, the transforming power of God set me free during my freshman year in college. I was a pre-med major with a swimming scholarship that was quickly falling apart when His grace appeared. God spoke bold words of love, value, and faithfulness through the Holy Spirit. He said, "I have more for you than this," and beckoned me to respond to His leading. It was a way out. I had to start anew. It was so scary and yet so freeing.

Even today, after fifteen years of marriage, I continue to battle the lies of inferiority, rejection, and shame. Still, He has allowed me to be both bold and humbly beautiful as his treasured daughter. Since I first heard the Spirit offer me a brand new way, that would mean the old would need to die. Psalm 40:2-3 NIV describes my testimony. "He lifted me out of the slimy pit, out of the mud and mire, He set my feet on a rock and gave me a firm place to stand. He put a new song in my mouth, a hymn of praise to our God. Many will see and fear and put their trust in the Lord."

Tonya's Story

"Tonya, on your sixteenth birthday, your father presented you with a ring. By accepting this ring, you vowed to remain pure until your wedding day. Did you keep that promise?"

"Yes," I replied.

"You may give the ring back to your father."

I took the ring off my finger and gave it to Daddy as the entire congregation erupted with "Praise God!" and "Amen!"

Daddy slipped the ring on his pinky finger, lifted my veil to kiss me on the cheek, and then gave me away to my beloved husband. I was twenty-one years old and experiencing my "happily ever after." It hadn't been easy, but here I stood on my wedding day in a white Cinderella wedding gown. The fact that my husband was a virgin also made it even more beautiful.

It was the happiest day of my life. I had made it. All my life, I had been warned to keep myself pure until marriage. "Stay pure... UNTIL marriage." Let that sink in. We need to stop telling young ladies to stay pure "until marriage" as if once you're married, you now have a license to engage in behavior and conversation that is impure. Instead, the charge should be to "keep yourself pure." Period. After all, sex within the confines of marriage *is* pure.

Satan has done such a good job of perverting sex that we've stopped recognizing marital sex as pure. And because of that, many married Christian women believe it is okay to engage in acts such as masturbation or watching pornography because "I'm married now. My purity has gone out the window along with my lonely days of being a single woman."

The danger in telling women to keep themselves pure *until* marriage is that after marriage, they tend to let their guard down and allow satan to come in. How do I know? Because it happened to me.

My marriage started out beautifully, but I didn't understand how vigorously satan attacks marriage. Because marriage is a direct representation of Christ and the church, satan has a personal vendetta against it. Sisters, don't look at marriage as the end all be all. Don't look at marriage as the destination that you are excited to reach because you can relax and have sex whenever you want. You won't have to practice as much restraint, right? Wrong.

Satan has done an excellent job of deceiving the church into believing that sexual sin is a "man's sin." Men are charged to guard their eyes and to be aware of falling into sexual sin. But who are they falling into sexual sin with? It isn't always the loose woman who is not in the church. It is often the woman who has a rich background in the church and the ways of God. It is often the woman who knows better but is a slave to her emotions, so she follows her feelings into the mire and becomes entrapped in a dangerous stronghold.

I took my purity and my walk with God for granted. I didn't strive to remain pure, and when the newness of being married and having sex wore off, I fell. Hard. After six years of being married, quite frankly, the "happily ever after" dwindled. My husband didn't compliment me like He used to. He didn't help me with the dishes, and He seemed more interested in watching football than spending time with me.

Our firstborn was two years old, and I was still toting around thirty-five pounds of baby weight. I didn't feel beautiful, and I didn't feel happy. In a word, I was miserable…until that fateful night. I was surfing Myspace, the popular social media site, at the time when I got a message in my inbox.

Hey, lady, how are you? It's been a long time.

My heart skipped a beat. It was James, the guy all the girls wanted to date back when I was in high school. I looked at his profile picture. After those years, He seemed to look even better.

I replied: *I'm fine, James. How are you?*

Our conversation continued and lasted for about thirty minutes. We talked about the old days when we were in high school, our hometown, and caught up on each other's lives. It was completely innocent. At least that's what I told myself.

My husband and I grew farther and farther apart. I couldn't believe it. How could this happen to us, the couple with the "perfect" start? Oh, how I wish I could go back in time and speak to twenty-seven-year-old Tonya. I'd tell her to fast and pray and to draw nigh to God. I'd tell her to pray for wisdom in finding a godly mentor, a prayer warrior who would challenge and uphold her. But I did not draw nigh to God; I drifted further away.

My conversations with James became more frequent. I looked forward to my husband going to bed each night, so I could log into Myspace and escape the stress of my marriage. One night, in particular, I was furious with my husband. James asked, *What's up?* And that's when I responded: *Nothing, I'm just a desperate housewife.*

That was all He needed to hear.

You're a desperate housewife? James typed. *Why? You're bored?*

Extremely bored, I replied.

James took it upon himself to dig a little deeper. He asked me a series of questions that soon turned sexual in nature. I was intrigued and flattered.

If you're bored, you can solve that with a little erotic conversation.

I was naïve and had no idea what exactly He meant.

Erotic conversation? I typed.

He replied: *Phone sex.*

I had never had phone sex before. I didn't understand how it worked. But James didn't hesitate to teach me. We began having phone sex every chance we got. I knew it was wrong. I felt dirty each time we finished, yet I longed for more. I was living a double life. I sang in the choir at church, I taught Sunday School and attended Bible Study, but behind closed doors, I was committing adultery.

My husband noticed something was wrong when we were intimate. Our connection was gone. He asked me over and over what was wrong, and I would just lie and say I was distracted with the many woes of being a stay-at-home mom.

Some days, I was so overwhelmed with conviction that I couldn't stand it. I'd pray and confess and feel empowered, but when James reached out to me, I was too weak to turn him down. I had never faced such strong sexual temptation. The two-year courtship with my husband had been a bit easier because He lived three hours away, and we only saw each other once or twice a month. When we did see each other, my parents were vigilant in holding us accountable and making sure we didn't spend too much alone time together. Even with all of those boundaries, we still found ways to cross them. Yes, we were virgins on our wedding day, but we certainly weren't perfect.

Even still, the temptation we faced prior to marriage was absolutely nothing compared to what I experienced *after* marriage. I simply couldn't resist James' flattering words and sexual advances. He lived an hour away but soon began asking me to visit him. He wanted more than phone sex. He wanted to consummate our adulterous relationship.

I made plans to visit him and told a friend who I knew would tell me everything I wanted to hear. After all, she wasn't that close to the Lord and was engaged in her own extramarital relationship. We were all set to leave together for a "girl's night" that would end up with both of us visiting our extramarital love interests. The day before our excursion, she called me.

"Tonya, we can't do this. We know better! What if we get found out? We just can't do this!"

The Holy Spirit used her words to convict me. I listened to her and told James that not only would I not be able to visit him, but we also couldn't have any contact anymore. He said He respected my decision.

I felt so good knowing that I didn't succumb to having sexual intercourse with anyone other than my husband. I prayed and put everything behind me. I went to bed that night with a sense of relief all over me. I had narrowly escaped a terrible situation.

Or had I? I woke in the wee hours of the morning, and my husband wasn't next to me. I could hear him in the other room on the computer. Anger flooded me. What was He doing on the computer? I decided to tiptoe into the living room to see what on earth He was doing on the computer at 4 am, but what I saw on the computer took my breath away. My husband was staring at every conversation I had with James. I thought I had deleted them all, but there they were on the computer monitor. I had been found out.

The days and weeks that followed were beyond painful. I watched my husband cry harder than I ever had. He was hurt and threatened to leave and take our daughter with him. I had to tell my family what was going on because I was certain I would have to move back home. After all, my husband was going to leave me. My mother was hurt; my father cried. It wasn't worth it. No matter what, it just wasn't worth it. My husband and I endured grueling counseling sessions and lots of hard days, but we pushed through and are still together fifteen plus years later.

Sisters, guard your hearts. Place your hopes, dreams, goals, and expectations in the hands of Jesus. As you practice purity in your everyday life, understand that you can never let your guard down. Not even as a wife.

Satan is out to kill, steal, and destroy each of us. None of us is any match for him. But here's the good news. Our God is greater. He is greater than your past. He is greater than your regrets, and He is greater than our vile enemy who seeks to ruin us.

Give God your purity, sisters. When you yield every part of yourself to Him, you experience contentment, joy, and strength. Let God fill every empty space in your life with Him. You will never want for anything again.

Sabrina's Story

Growing up in a home where you are told not to have sex can make you extremely inquisitive. You hear, "Don't bring any babies in this house." You hear, "It is going to hurt," and "Sex is for marriage." No more details are provided about sexual intercourse or the consequences that can come with that decision. No details are provided about the beauty of sex within a marital relationship.

In my mind, I thought, *What is the big deal?* I was in high school the first time I had premarital sex. The young man was not my boyfriend, but I desired him to be. He took me upstairs behind the gym and promised that He wanted to be with me. It was a horrible experience. It hurt, and it was awkward. He didn't ask me to be his girlfriend but wanted to continue having sex with me. I agreed a few more times, and this opened the door to my sex life. It's crazy when I think about it. A teenage girl should not be able to say she has a sex life. My parents tried to tell me, but they were not completely open, so I wanted to see for myself.

I felt rejected after that sexual experience, and even though the young man did not accept me as his girlfriend, He continued to come to me for sex. I believed that you had to have sex with men in order for them to love you. I now know that sex is not love, but for a very long time, I lived my life thinking that sex was love.

Premarital sex will never give you love. Premarital sex will make you lose a little piece of yourself with each experience. You lose self-worth and self-esteem and a small piece of your heart with each transaction. Inside, I felt like I was something special each time someone wanted to sleep with me. I wasn't anything special. I also felt like men don't think you are special; they just want sex. Plain and simple! As a young lady, even as a grown woman, we get emotionally connected because of how God created us. Women are emotional creatures, and men are emotionally detached. You think you are in love, and the man is seeking the fastest exit.

Freedom was a long and hard journey for me. When you live a life of promiscuity, your mind and body are in bondage. Freedom comes when you learn to forgive yourself for bad decisions. Bad decisions are not the end of life, but if you allow them to continue, they will destroy your mind. A destroyed mind will lead to allowing men to have their way with your body while controlling your mind.

Freedom came for me from learning how much God loves me and then allowing Him to love me. We have free will. God was always there, but I was absent. Even in freedom, mistakes happen, so I had to learn how to repent and believe that I was forgiven for my mistakes. Freedom also came with me loving myself. Loving yourself first will open up your eyes. Open eyes produce better decision making.

During this process, I learned that God loves me unconditionally and sent His son to die on the cross, even for my sexual sins. At times, I would categorize sins and sex outside of marriage, and it seemed unforgivable, but God, through His Word, taught me that He forgives all sin. He is faithful and just in everything, and He has healed so much within me. God taught me that He gave me my story because He created me, and my story is not just for me. It is to help heal someone else.

God took me in His arms and taught me what real love was supposed to feel like and look like. He taught me that no one could ever love me like Him, not even my earthly father. God showed Himself to me during the process by blocking doors. I had hookups planned that fell through. That was God! God will keep you and bring you out looking like the queen He created.

Life was challenging for me because I was looking for love. Thinking that sex was love, I can truly say I was looking for sex. Dealing with a bunch of sexual relationships can hinder you when you meet the person you truly love. The mind plays tricks on you, and you always wonder, *is sex all this person wants from me?*

Healing is important because that baggage travels with you everywhere you go. Don't allow hurts from the past, bad decision making, and early sexual relationships to hinder your marriage. Don't allow bad things that others have asked you to do to haunt you in your marriage forever. Don't put all men in the same position. They are not all the same.

If I were able to give my little princess inside some advice, I would tell her:

- God loves you more than anyone will ever love you in your life.

- Listen to your parents.

- Don't grow up too fast.

- Enjoy your friends in groups.

- Don't allow any young man to touch you.

- Don't let anyone make you feel pressured to have sex.

- Love yourself just the way you are.

- Sex is beautiful between a husband and wife, and you'll want to save yourself for that relationship.

- Premarital sex has many consequences that can affect you for the rest of your life.

Serra's Story

I didn't expect what would happen to me at nine years old in a side room of my aunt's home with my fifteen-year-old cousin. My mother and aunt, this cousin's mother, were both in the living room talking, and we decided to play operation. I remember lying on the bed by a window that was facing my grandfather's house. I knew something was wrong, but I did not stop it. From that day on, for years, I chased that feeling that was birthed over thirty-five years ago.

Unaware of the damage done at the time, I believed this touch was going to make me secure, attended to, and wanted. I began touching family members who were my age to experience that feeling again. At the age of fifteen, I gave in to peer pressure with a schoolmate I didn't even know well. Shamefully, that was my first experience that crossed every sexual boundary. I remember all of his friends being downstairs in his house, and He and I somehow ended upstairs when one thing led to another. This encounter turned into widespread news at school that I had "given it up." It was humiliating, to say the least.

A couple of months later, I entered a relationship with a guy that lasted almost seven years. He was my first love and my first heartbreak. After all that time, He cheated, and all of my dreams were shattered. When I contracted chlamydia four years into our relationship, I never once thought that He may have been cheating. The truth was I did not know if I contracted this STD from the first guy or this boyfriend. Sad but true. After taking medication, it cleared up, and I continued in the relationship. I thought we were going to get married, but we did not. I was so hurt and lost. I did not know who I was. I did not feel secure anymore.

Consequently, I went on a journey to find love again. I did whatever it took to fill the emptiness inside without thinking about the repercussions. I was lost and felt like I needed to be found by someone who cherished me as my ex-boyfriend did for all those years. Searching, I went from man to man, lying with them to find security but always got up empty. Little did I know, security could not be found aside from my loving God, who created me perfectly for His good work, not for someone else's dirty pleasure.

In the midst of all these encounters, I became involved with a guy who was temporarily working in town. He became my boyfriend before He left town again on another venture with his job. A few weeks after He left for his prolonged work trip, I found myself pregnant. I was shocked when I took the pregnancy test. *Positive? No, please, Lord, No!*

Reality hit, and I decided that abortion was going to be the escape route from the consequences of my sins. I could not go back home with a child in my stomach. I knew that if I went home pregnant, I would be found out by everyone that mattered to me — my family, my friends, and my church members. I feared their responses, the looks on their faces, and their wagging fingers in judgment, implying, "I told you so."

Abortion was the final answer, and yes, what you are thinking is correct. I sacrificed my own child for the sake of preserving my own *perceived* reputation. Terrible decision, I know—the worst one I have ever made. The thing is, I wanted to look the Christian part, especially to my family and church members, because being an unmarried pregnant college student was unacceptable. It would have brought shame and embarrassment to my family. My church may have wanted me to come before the congregation to confess, and I could not even imagine myself going through that. Four years prior to this, the church had already asked a teenager to stand up and tell the church she was pregnant, so that was a situation I never wanted to encounter myself.

I contacted the father of the baby and told him what was going on. He sent money for half of the cost of the abortion. My best friend took me to the clinic, and the surgical procedure went faster than I expected. I was in pain but relieved that I did not have to face the world with a big belly.

Weeks later, my boyfriend told me He wished I had not aborted our baby but understood the reasons I felt I had to proceed with this option. I never knew I would feel this way, but I regret the decision completely. Today, I realize that I may have aborted the only child I would ever have. Although I lived many years dismissing the existence of my daughter's short life (I think my baby was a girl), I am now happy to say that I live with the gift of sorrow. This feeling allows me to honor her very short purpose in the world and reminds me that we can never escape sin. It has eternal consequences.

Several years later, I re-dedicated my life to the Lord. As years went by, I learned how to conduct my relationships with the opposite sex in a godly way without crossing physical boundaries. Today, I have been abstinent for almost nineteen years. It has not been easy. This lifestyle has caused me to choose accountability partners who can hold me to my commitment of setting boundaries while in the presence of men and having conversations with them. These ladies pray for me and remind me of the purposes God has for me. I have had to pray more often, give my frustrations and hormonal urges to the Lord, change the music I listen to and movies I watch, and reconsider the time I spend with certain friends who do not share the same lifestyle. I have done a lot that was the opposite of God's best for me, but today I can say that I'm living for Him with passion and full devotion.

Today, if I were talking to my younger self, I would say, "Be encouraged. Trust that the Lord has great plans and purposes for your life. He loves you and will not harm you. Even if you mess up, go to Father God and talk to Him about it. He is on your side. He will strengthen you and hold you by your right hand so that you don't go down the wrong path again.

"God cares about your sex drive. He cares about all you are dealing with. He does not want you to feel lonely or worthless. He wants to be your Almighty Companion, who keeps you company, makes you laugh, and fulfills your life with plans beyond your wildest dreams. He walks with you closer than a brother or a sister.

"You have everything you need when you are with Him. He will take you on adventures and surprise you with your favorite things. God has put a stamp of value on your life and a label of great worth. Both can never be removed.

"He sent His Son Jesus, who died for you and will probably be the only One in this lifetime who will ever die for you. You can count on God to always be there in every situation. He will not leave you or forsake you. Jehovah God always provides, and as you wait on Him, He will strengthen you for everything He has destined for you. You will never find another Lover better than Him.

Teka's Story

I was raised in a rigorous Christ-centered, single-parent home under the leadership of my mother. I was molested as a child from the age of about five until I was a preteen by multiple family members, although I only remember two or three. Aside from experiencing molestation, I was a virgin until I went to college, where I met my ex-fiancé. The second time I had ever had sex was with him. The first time was out of pressure from a guy I dated as a freshman. I literally did it to please him and had no desire to participate. Prior to going to college, I felt like all men were dogs because my mom pretty much set that tone in my head as an angry single mother of three. From childhood, I never really had a healthy respect for men.

There came a time in my life where I felt like I could be delivered from all other sins except fornication. I would abstain for a while and then fall and then abstain for some time and fall again. I didn't realize the reason I kept failing was because I was lonely and desired companionship and intimacy. What I thought was love was really lust. I kept thinking I could get a man to fall in love with me through the bedroom, test driving before a marital commitment, and releasing myself of the abstinence stress, but I was sadly mistaken. I never had an issue meeting and dating men, but I had a serious issue when it came to allowing my flesh to be in control instead of yielding to the Holy Spirit.

I was creating a plethora of soul ties and emotional attachments that masked my real desire for marriage. Each shallow, lust-filled relationship deepened my disappointment and delayed the fulfillment of my purpose-driven life. With spiritual blinders on and earplugs firmly fixed in place, I was giving in to self-sabotage, malfunctioning my spiritual authority, and aborting my blessings. This lifestyle opened demonic doors that tried to forfeit my destiny.

I decided I would only date for marriage and entered into a long-term relationship unexpectedly. About twenty-one years prior, we had been in a committed relationship in college. After reconnecting and recommitting to our relationship, once again, I fell into fornication. Two years in, the relationship grew more serious, and my mindset was stuck on the fact that we were getting married anyway, so I rationalized continuing to have sex.

As I matured in my Christian walk, I began feeling the conviction of the Holy Spirit. It dawned on me that God did not bless sin, and I decided if I wanted the approval and blessing of God on my marriage, I would have to stop sinning. Fornication was no longer an option.

This shift occurred during my last engagement. I received my engagement ring the morning after we had sex. It wasn't a formal proposal. The ring was absolutely gorgeous, but the proposal was not what I expected. It felt like it came from a sense of obligation instead of genuine love.

With only four months between the proposal and the wedding date, I went through the motions of wedding planning with my type A personality and very selective style. I had all the bases covered with the purchase of my dress, veil, bridesmaids' accessories, deposits made on the venue, caterer, and was about to move on to the deposit for the band. Then, I realized I needed a deeper understanding of whether this was really the will of God. I was not at peace about moving forward because my then fiancé had exhibited some unsettling, negative behaviors.

I felt I heard God say not to move forward. I told my bridesmaids to return their dresses, and if they did not receive a refund, I would pay them back. I had eleven bridesmaids, but I wasn't concerned about the monetary repercussions or losing my deposits. I feared divorce from an unblessed marriage. I feared being with the wrong person and not receiving the royal treatment. I felt that He wasn't ready for marriage, although later, I found I too had some areas to tighten up myself.

Selfishness was an issue for both of us. We both had strong personalities, and I didn't realize how controlling I could be. I had been a real boss for many years. Since college, I was in high-ranking leadership positions in both the military and corporate sectors. I needed to learn to respect and honor him as my husband, even though I was making more money. To this day, I am very grateful I did not move forward.

The fact that I received the ring was indicative of his desire to be with me, and I appreciated that. But, I also understood that I needed to feel secure in his ability to lead in our marriage and in our lives as a Christ-centered home. I believed in submission with my husband as the head, but I realized I didn't respect his leadership. I didn't feel He had enough spiritual authority over any demonic activity that would come for our marriage.

In that process with my now ex-fiancé, although it was difficult to undo all the wedding planning, I did not fear being alone. I saw the red flags in our relationship and did not ignore them. I took the risk of embarrassment and decided that I wasn't going to go through with the wedding and put on a façade. Besides, too many people were saying marriage was overrated and things go south after the vows. I looked at God's track record in my life and felt He had a more suitable mate for me.

The enemy always made me feel like my biological clock was ticking, and I was running out of time and would not meet the man of my dreams.

Today, I would tell my younger self that no matter how much I was fondled as a child, I was still pure, and I should not allow anyone to rob me of that, nor should I rob myself of it. Soul ties result from having sex, and they have a major negative impact on your mental and emotional well-being. I used to believe that the men telling me they loved me were being honest, but it was really deception to get me to sleep with them. I believed I didn't have the willpower to wait for marriage and that I had already lost my virginity, so it no longer mattered.

Let's face it. Sex is addictive. My mom would always say, "Don't ever start having sex because if you start, you won't want to stop." I believe that, and I believe in saving sex for marriage because of the repercussions of soul ties. There are scriptures that speak against sexual immorality and how disobedience brings curses in our lives.

I learned that God REALLY DOES love us unconditionally. His grace and mercy are MORE THAN sufficient. He forgives us well before we forgive ourselves, and He knows when we will sin before it even occurs. He will also STILL use us to do the work even when we don't feel like we're really free from bondage. In fact, there was a time in my younger Christian walk where He used me mightily in the church despite my weaknesses. I am a living testimony that "gifts and callings come without repentance," which has also given me a sense of compassion and empathy toward others who fall short.

Fornication has allowed me to learn a lot about men and their behaviors. It also allowed me to experience the emotional and psychological impact of soul ties. I've taken on personalities of men who were extremely broken themselves and, as a result, brought a level of brokenness in me. It took years to get free from the demons that bound them. Those demons impacted other relationships in my life and often left me feeling emotional and full of void.

Desperation definitely pushed me closer to God in pursuit of being whole and holy. It taught me the importance of being in a real covenant with God. If I couldn't be in covenant with Him, He would never trust me to be in covenant with someone He has chosen for me. It caused me to level up in how I viewed myself as a future wife, not just as a girlfriend. As a single woman, I now believe that I have options and don't need to feel rushed into a commitment or settle for a man who can't accommodate God's vision for my life.

You Can Do This!

Dear Sisters, just hearing the stories of those courageous women should give you confidence that you, too, can be transformed by taking this journey one step at a time. When you find yourself struggling in a certain area, go back and review the chapters, follow the guidelines, and pray the prayers again. You can use this like a manual so you can apply it to the areas where you need it the most.

Believe by faith that you will turn that corner and get back on the right track. There is another side to where you are right now. This is the hope you need. Listen, God wants this transformation for you so if you want it, you will inevitably come into a new lifestyle and accomplish the purposes already set for your life.

Now, will this process be over in a day, a month, or even a year? Maybe. Maybe not. But let me tell you this one thing: YOU CAN DO THIS and I know you can because I have been there. At first, I did not think I could do it, but I did. My heart desired to please God and remain pure, but my behavior would communicate the exact opposite. I am so glad God looks on the heart (I Samuel 16:7b, ESV). I was looking on the outward appearance and would tell anyone that I could never successfully walk in purity. It was a battle, but it was also a battle worth fighting because I won the war, y'all.

I won because the Bible says I am MORE than a conquer in Christ Jesus who loves me (Romans 8:37, NIV), and today I am doing the very thing I thought I could not do. I am free! And you can be too.

Yes, it will take hard work, resistance, and humility. You will have to make tough decisions. Some of these decisions may feel like losses in the beginning, but they are not. Don't believe that lie. Stay focused on the goal of pleasing God and walking in purity and freedom. This will give you the peace that passes all understanding (Philippians 4:7, ESV).

The big decisions you make now will allow you to reap great rewards in the future. DON'T GIVE UP!

You've got this. You have everything in you right now to live the life you have always wanted to live. There will be times when you feel like it is impossible. You may wonder if you are the only one on the purity journey. Sometimes, it will feel lonely, and to be perfectly honest, you may not hear a lot of people around you pursuing a lifestyle of abstinence or applauding you because you are choosing it. But I am here to tell you that as you take the hand of Almighty God and as you commit to live a life of purity from this day forward, even when you get married, you will gain traction and see yourself press toward the mark of the high calling in Christ Jesus. Heaven is applauding you and I am cheering you on!

My prayer is that you find freedom from the bondage of sexual sin and experience a transformation in your mind, body, soul, and spirit. I do not doubt that I will hear from you when you believe the same and start walking it out. Make sure you tell me how your journey is going.

Today, I commission you to pursue purity in your mind, body, and soul. There is an entire generation of girls waiting for you. Now go in faith and trust that God is already working powerfully in you. You will surprise yourself as you join the movement and commit to the journey of Stepping Into Purity...and beyond.

"[Now] May the God of peace Himself make you entirely pure and devoted to God;
and may your spirit and soul and body be kept strong and blameless until that day
when our Lord Jesus Christ comes back again."

More About the Author

Vernicia T. Eure has obtained a Master of Arts in Human Services Counseling and a Bachelor of Science in Administrative Systems. She is also a Certified Traumatologist with the Green Cross School of Traumatology and has a year of post-graduate studies in Strategic Leadership. Vernicia has over 16 years of experience in management and currently serves as Client Services Director at a pregnancy medical clinic in Northern Virginia. She assists with the hiring process and is responsible for supervising and training the counseling, medical and administrative staff, and volunteers in Client Services.

As President and Founder of S.T.E.P. Consulting Group LLC, Vernicia uses her passion for having a personal relationship with the Lord coupled with leadership, counseling, and public speaking to influence audiences in the U.S. and abroad.

Vernicia is also the Founder of the Stepping Into Purity and Beyond Group (on Facebook) and the Author of Stepping Into Purity's 12-Step Incubator Program (12-SIP), a six-week group coaching program for single women. 12-SIP is designed to be a practical guide for women to deepen their relationship with God, break soul ties from unhealthy relationships, create boundaries in dating, and form accountability partnerships with other SIP sisters who have committed to the purity journey. Through her products and services, Vernicia is dedicated to empowering single women to reclaim their identity in Christ by overcoming the fear of being alone, knowing their purpose, and making wiser selections in the dating process. Schedule your free discovery consultation at www.verniciateure.com.